I0568243

The Master's Piece

The Master's Piece

AUTO-BIOGRAPHY OF SYLVIA BENSON

SYLVIA BENSON

Merrill
PUBLISHING

Copyright © 2022 J Merrill Publishing, Inc.

All rights reserved. No part of this publication may be reproduced, distributed, or transmitted in any form or by any means, including photocopying, recording, or other electronic or mechanical methods, without the prior written permission of the publisher, except in the case of brief quotations embodied in critical reviews and certain other noncommercial uses permitted by copyright law. For permission requests, write to the publisher, addressed "Attention: Permissions Coordinator," at the address below.

J Merrill Publishing, Inc.
434 Hillpine Drive
Columbus, OH 43207
www.JMerrill.pub

Library of Congress Control Number: 2022908069
ISBN-13: 978-1-954414-48-8 (Paperback)
ISBN-13: 978-1-954414-47-1 (eBook)

Book Title: The Master's Piece
Author: Sylvia Benson
Editor: Ceaphrael Benson

Contents

CHAPTER 1

Her Family

"And we know that all things work together for good to them that love God, to them who are the called according to his purpose."

— *ROMANS 8:28*

At the age of seventeen, a prophet told Evon L. Mackey that she would possess something more extraordinary than silver or gold. Unbeknown to her, that possession was in the form of a child she named Sylvia Lynn Mackey. She was born July 9, 1967, at OSU Hospital in Columbus, Ohio. Sylvia entered into a large family as the first grandchild. Being born into a family full of preachers, serving God was instilled in her early. Her grandfather was the founder and pastor of A.O.H. (Apostolic Original Holy Church of God), where he and her grandmother served faithfully.

Two years later, Sylvia was joined by her first brother and became the eldest of seven children as time went on. They didn't have a whole lot of money, but they had a lot of love. Evon raised her children to respect, love, cherish one another, and most importantly, to serve God. Often, Sylvia would have to watch her siblings so that Evon could work to provide for them all. Sylvia seemed to develop quicker than the girls her age. Because of it, she could have very easily passed for an older woman.

Despite how shy Sylvia was, God had gifted her with the most precious gift, and that was the ability to sing. No matter how often or where, come what may, she was going to sing! Sylvia and her siblings were grandchildren of the founders of their place of worship. Which meant they were raised to be fully multifaceted in all things church.

Religiously, they were sweeping the floors and starting the morning services.

Sylvia's family was huge on being holy. Things like worldly music and partying were not allowed. Luckily, Sylvia adored God and loved going to church, so it was a thrill for her to abide by holiness and attend church regularly. At her church, she received Christ at the early age of eleven and was always reminded that God had a unique plan for her life. There would be several times when she'd become ill but would try to hide it from her mother out of fear of potentially missing an opportunity to worship.

Sylvia and her siblings were very close. They made sure that they protected one another. Along with the sibling love and protection, the church just so happened to be a family church where lots of cousins, uncles, and aunts were all faithful members. They became the only friends they had and the only friends they needed. There were a lot of dinners at the church, especially on Sundays. There was no doubt we were a traditional, black church. Services would be from 9:30 am until 10:00 pm.

Sylvia's grandfather was her hero. Not only was he a fantastic pastor, but he was also a Mason and a farmer! Her grandfather, her uncle, and other church members would build the sanctuaries from the ground up. He had cows, goats, chickens, pigs, horses, and even bulls on his farm! Boy! It seemed as though he grew the biggest crops in all of Licking County. His work was so great that people would often come and admire his produce and his livestock. In addition, he was the only father that Sylvia knew at that time in her life.

Before we go on, I'd hate to prolong further your well-earned anticipation for what you may go on to discover and unpack. However, I must pause for the cause and intentionally defy all the laws of literature as I abruptly shift from a Third-Person Point of View briefly into a Second-Person Point of View. Now, this is only to welcome you, the reader, of course. What you are entering into may be similar to what you've once felt, heard of, or experienced. I applaud you today for being open-minded and for being brave enough to insert yourself into another perspective. Now follow me as I actively assume the First-Person Point of View. If you hadn't guessed by now, I am Sylvia L. Mackey, presently known as Sylvia Benson (we'll get into that here shortly.) I come to present myself not as the character, the protagonist, or the antagonist, but only as The Master's Piece.

CHAPTER 2
School Days

"For I know the plans I have for you," says the Lord. "They are plans for good and not for disaster, to give you hope and a future."

— JEREMIAH 29:11

As the years advanced, my siblings continued to grow, and the responsibility of watching them started to feel overwhelming. I was fully aware that taking care of them was to alleviate the pressure off of my mother. However, the cost of it all held me back from a year in my education. Even still, I loved school, which made it easy to maintain good grades. While attending grade school, the students often had difficulty grasping that I, too, was a student and not a teacher.

While residing in the small city of Pataskala, my mother decided it was time for a change in location into the city. We became accustomed to living in the country where there were mostly Caucasians. Meaning we were able to leave our doors unlocked and maintain excellent relationships with our neighbors. Imagine the culture shock we experienced once transitioning into the city. It felt like we dropped into the hands of the enemy! Not only did we have to lock our doors, but locking the windows and closets started to feel like a good idea too. In total, it took about a year for my siblings and me to adjust fully. I can remember us moving to Boulevard Arms in Columbus, OH (which happened to be one of the worst areas in the city,) and we were only able to stay there for three short weeks. One day, my mother walked my brother and me from school, and as we approached the apartment, we quickly realized we were being robbed in broad daylight! We saw the thieves leaving through the window with our TV, dressers, and groceries! One of them dared to tell us, "Thank you for everything!"

My mother called my grandfather and told him what had taken place, and by the end of that week, we were moving!

I am now in seventh grade and attending one of my favorite schools, Indianola Junior High School. My favorite teacher was Mrs. Staples, my music teacher. Mrs. Staples made sure to spoil me by constantly pulling me out of class to assist her with other students regarding music. I always admired the way that she dressed, smelled, and how she wore her hair. She became a great role model for me to follow. While in seventh grade, I was dating a guy from church who was about three years older than me. The guys who were my age just weren't mature enough for my liking.

But one day, I heard of a cute guy who had just transferred from another school named Thomas Antoine Benson. He was called "Twan." He was very handsome, charming, and funny. Twan later became my previous husband and the father of all my children. However, he was a playboy. I secretly watched Twan throughout each day claim his territories by putting his signature "playboy" necklace around each girl's neck. I became quickly annoyed with my fascination. But I couldn't help that I was intrigued. I didn't say anything because I was timid. My next thought isn't to say that the "church" can't be worldly, but I tried my best to refrain from Twan, who was *clearly* of the world.

Two months had gone by since the incomparable "Twan" had transferred to Indianola, and we had finally spoken. I happened to be standing in the line in front of him to get my lunch, and he asked, "Are you a teacher? And if so, what class do you teach?" I responded with, "No, I'm a student."

Him being the clown he was, he responded, "OH YEAH?!" (In his Morris Day voice.) "Well, can I get them seven digits?!"

Shockingly, I told him, "Yes."

That evening, Twan called me and began asking me different questions like, "Do you have a boyfriend?" And I let him know not anymore because the guy I was talking to was a "playboy" also. He then went on to ask me if I was allowed to go out anywhere. I told him that I was a church girl and didn't like guys who didn't go to church. He responded with, "Hallelujah, I'm saved!"

The next day, Twan asked me to be his girlfriend, and I quickly accepted! The girls were jealous already, so this new connection made them even more upset. We lasted as a couple for two whole weeks (which was a record because you only got to hold that title for one week). Twan ended things by writing me a note stating that although he liked me a lot and loved my singing, he could no longer go out with me because his mom was forcing him to end things. Twan was already so unique to only be in the seventh grade, but this was too much! Of course, the next day, he had a new girlfriend. But I couldn't stay mad at him for too long. After the breakup, I would still speak to him, although he could barely look me in the face the majority of the time.

CHAPTER 3
Linden McKinley

"Therefore, if any man be in Christ, he is a new creature: old things are passed away; behold, all things are become new."

— *2 CORINTHIANS 5:17*

Being too content in an environment makes change all the more challenging, nevertheless, inevitable. The thought of having to go from middle school to high school became extremely nerve-racking to my very developed, twelve-year-old self. As an eighth-grader, I had heard so many stories about upper-level students preying on the freshman class. Showing up with clothes that were out of style was considered detestable. Not having the latest fashion caused great anxiety for me at the time. Especially seeing how aware I was that my body forced me to stand out from most of my peers in middle school, I was nervous about how this would affect me in high school. On top of it all, there was a program by the name of Charity Newsies. Charity Newsies was a service where workers would come to your home and sort through our clothes to see how many coats, sweaters, shirts, and shoes they had and what condition they were in. Due to the number of kids my mother had, we were signed up annually for this program. My siblings and I hated it because all of the clothes we would receive looked alike, making it evident that they came from Charity Newsies. This made my anxiety about going to high school worse.

I attended Linden McKinley High School. Oh, how proud I was to attend a school with a name that carried such class and poise! It was so exciting to see just how different high school was from middle school. All of the kids looked so mature compared to the younger grades. Plus, the building?! It was double the size of the building I had just left, making the process of getting to my classes a pretty tricky task for the first two weeks.

It didn't take long for me to gain the "*The Church Girl*" title, seeing that I had already marked my place in the choir. Everyone knew that I could sing because I was constantly humming throughout my day. While navigating through high school, I kept being approached by guys wanting relationships with me. But seeing as though I had my fair share of not-so-great relationships before coming to high school, I wasn't that thrilled by the idea of another one. Especially considering the older church boy I had previously pursued became a pretty popular football player and began bragging to me about all the girls who desired him. Regardless of his unwarranted efforts at trying to intimidate me, relationships just weren't a priority at that time in my life. In my regret for giving myself away to him, I knew I needed to pause on romance and pursue healthy friendships only. It was not long before I had met a pleasant girl by the name of Cassandra. After a few conversations, I discovered that she, too, was as churchy as I was. It seemed as if we had become best friends overnight, which was incredibly refreshing.

As time went on, I began to hear about this monumental event in the form of a talent show called the "Masterpiece." After hearing many conversations about the event, I discovered people gathered from all over Columbus to witness this event. Possibly being a part of the talent show flirted with my artistic self tremendously, as I had never participated in something like this before. But after much-needed encouragement from my newfound friend and my music teacher, I decided to go for it. Above all, I was most nervous about having to sing a secular song. I had no idea how my mother and family would take that, considering that all I had ever performed was gospel music. However, the feeling I had when my music teacher told me I could sing anything?! It was irreplaceable! That's when I decided to perform "And I Am Telling You" by Jennifer Holiday. I'd spent time in a practice room at my school leading up to the big day. Kids often would come and peak in or stand at the windows near the room to listen. It was the discovery of my talent that led to the discovery of me.

CHAPTER 4

Lights, Camera, Action

YOUR DEFINING MOMENT

After an overwhelming day of excitement, the final step was telling my mom about the talent show. Surprisingly enough, she granted me approval to participate in the talent show! After overcoming that obstacle, it took me a few days longer to tell her exactly what song I had planned on singing. Once I mustered the courage to tell her the song's name, she assumed it was a gospel song which made me even happier. To see my mother showing interest in what I was doing made my heart smile. Not to say that she hadn't let me participate in choir concerts before; it's just that this time was different. My mom took this opportunity to boast to everyone she knew about how her daughter was to perform in a big showcase. She went as far as making an announcement in front of the entire church about it! I just knew I'd pass out after hearing her go on and on about what was to come. It was a ticketed event, so once the news got around about how special the occasion was, it seemed as though everyone was itching for a ticket.

As time began to fly ahead of me, I began to worry about what I would wear. That's when I remembered that one of the members of my church had made a gorgeous white and silver gown with a cape to match. My excitement continued rising with each day that passed. Along with that excitement came lots of nervousness. By practicing every day and constantly praying that I'd win, I could combat the little bit of fear I felt growing.

Throughout the days while being at school, Cassandra and I often sat and conversed about our lives. We'd often discussed our family issues, along with things we wished we could change. One day, in particular, she asked me how come I'd always talk about my mother but never my father. I told her that I didn't know who my father was. She went on to ask a few more questions, including if I at least knew his name. And the answer to that question was "no" as well. Being an intuitive friend, Cassandra suggested that I ask my mother what my dad's name was. I was quickly intrigued with the idea of putting a name to a mysterious man I hadn't heard too much of known to be my father. So, I told her I'd think about it.

Preparation for the Masterpiece was more than exceptional. Linden McKinley created flyers and made posters, along with announcing on the radio. In conjunction with my mother advertising in her way, all of this made for a very excited me. There were two mandatory dress rehearsals scheduled in preparation for the show. But Friday night was go-time, and it could not come fast enough. Other females were to participate in the show that tried their best to intimidate me. However, I remained focused on what was to come. My church family continuously prayed for me during that week, for which I was more than grateful.

At last, the day had come, and I was more anxious than I had ever been.

Completing any work at school that day was a task within itself. As the end of the workday slowly approached, the bell finally rang for us to go home, and I'm sure I was the first one out of the door. There was no eating or talking on the phone for me once I got home. I didn't want any distractions from what was to come for me that evening. Just as excited as I was, my mother sat me down and fixed my hair. She even let me wear some of her fine jewelry, which was a thrill. It was evident that the excitement became contagious throughout my home. After a while, my siblings even caught the emotion as if they had caught the Holy Ghost. They were constantly talking and humming the song that I was to sing that evening. And rightfully so, I mean, I had practiced it so much that I'm sure anyone in my home could've performed it.

As we approached the final stages of my preparation, it was time to put on the gown that was beautifully made just for me. At that moment, I couldn't help but take it all in. I took a beat to bask in the essence of how I looked, the way I felt, the time I had spent in preparation leading up to this point, and what was to come in just a few short moments. All of this must have gotten to my head a little. Because once it was time to go, I didn't want anyone to sit close to me out of fear of my dress potentially dirtying. My school was only a fifteen-minute drive from home, but it seemed to take hours to get there.

Nevertheless, we arrived. My family and I proceeded to get out of the station wagon, only to walk up the stairs to see all of my family and church members waiting with flowers and balloons! There were at least thirty of them, all there for me. The love and support that awaited me were breathtaking and highly overwhelming, and ultimately the perfect spark I needed right before showtime.

As my family went one way, I went the other to head backstage. The excitement that radiated behind the curtains was even more of an adrenaline rush. We had some students reporting to us how crowded it got out in the auditorium. Others were running back and forth, some were crying already, and a handful of us waited in anticipation.

Once the instructor began signaling things would start soon, my knees began to tremble, but I was ready. Moments later, the crowd started to roar, and that let me know that it was showtime! We that were backstage heard the Master of Ceremony say, "Welcome to the Masterpiece." And the crowd broke out into thunderous applause.

The acts for the evening began being called one by one, name by name. After each performance, everyone could hear the crowd cheering for their favorite person. And so far, everyone had been putting forth their best. Then the time came; it was my turn.

The MC announced my name, the curtains flew open, and suddenly it was lights, camera, and action! At that moment, time had taken a brief pause, and it was as if I had escaped my body. I had never felt what I felt right there in that space. The lights had taken a personal relationship with the color of my skin and the reflection of my gown. Everything familiar had seeped away from me. Face by face, chair by chair, each person sat in anticipation for whatever I chose to do next. It was all eyes on me, and every ear waited to hear what was to escape from me. As I looked over to see my music teacher sitting on the piano, waiting to give me my cue, I snapped back into reality. While hearing my name echoed throughout the auditorium from the mouths of my supporters, my teacher nodded at me, and it was showtime!

By the time the first note escaped my lungs, it seemed like the energy of the night had taken flight to an entirely different level, full of yelling, screaming, cheers, and crying! Although the song was approximately eight minutes long, it seemed as though only seconds had passed! Once the song was over, I took a bow, waved at the crowd, and returned backstage to await the winners' announcement. At this point, I was numb with excitement and anxiety for what was to come. After every act had gone, the MC finally announced the third runner-up, the second-place act, and lastly, the winner. A vast drum roll came about, and the MC went on to say, "And the moment you've all been waiting for, this year's Linden McKinley's winner for The Masterpiece is Sylvia Mackey!" Almost instantly, the crowd went nuts. Between the lights and the sound of roaring, I thought that I was going to pass out! Within a short couple of hours, I had experienced feelings that I would remember for the rest of my life, all under the lights, camera, and action!

CHAPTER 5
A Great Discovery

The weekend had passed, and another school day had begun. I was still on a high from winning the "Masterpiece," but I knew it was time to refocus on school. My friend Cassandra had written me a note that said, "I can't wait until lunch so we can talk!" That period seemed to have been dragging by. In the class, you could still hear students and teachers reminiscing over the weekend. Finally, the bell rang, and I headed to the cafeteria for lunch. While walking throughout the school to my various destinations, some students were cheering, and others were giving me dirty looks, which didn't matter. I felt good about myself, and I stood on that feeling. Cassandra and I sat down, and immediately she began to talk, laugh, and cry at the same time. That was the unique thing about Cassandra; she'd always tear up no matter what we were talking about, good or bad. Her next question was what my mother and church family said about me singing a secular song at the talent show. I told her that everyone loved the performance and made a huge announcement about it at church, which she thought was great! A few moments of silence passed, and Cassandra asked, "Did you ask your mom what your father's name is?"

I looked at her and said, "I haven't yet."

She responded with, "I think that you should find out because every girl should know who her father is." Her innocence and sincerity kept me smiling.

I told her, "I will think about asking my mom when the time is right."

For the rest of the day, I couldn't help but think about the words my friend had spoken to me. I honestly had not given much thought to what my father may have been like until Cassandra first asked me a few weeks back. But the more I thought about it, the more I wanted to know. That evening, my mother came to my room to check in on me.

But before she left the room, I stopped her and said, "Can I ask you a question?"

She said, "What is it?"

With slight hesitation, I asked, "Could you tell me what my father's name is?"

She paused and asked me why. I told her I'd been thinking about it lately and just really desired to know. She proceeded to tell me my father's name. I then asked, "Is he dead or alive?"

She says, "As far as I know, he's alive."

My heart began to beat so fast, and my mind began to wander to places it had never been. But I proceeded to ask more about my father. My mom said that she had met him at a concert; that she began following him and his group around to various churches throughout Columbus, Ohio. Mother told me that our church would fellowship with their church from time to time. And after a while, my father approached her and asked her what her name was, and she told him. Sometime after that, the both of them met out one night, then she never saw him again. I thanked my mom for sharing so much with me. I stood incredibly shocked at how much she shared. Following our conversation, I lay in bed for a while, thinking of everything I had learned. It was so neat to have found out all of the things that my father could do. He sang and played the piano, organ, and guitar. That meant that on both sides of my family, I had musical jeans. At this point, I could not wait to get to school the next day to tell Cassandra all that I had discovered about my dad. Strangely enough, I felt a new sense of worth that I had never felt before. All in one moment, I had gained something I didn't even realize I was missing until that evening.

The following day, I was the first one dressed and ready to get off to school. As I arrived, Cassandra was walking in at the same time as I was. As soon as I saw her, I said, "I asked my mom!"

She exclaimed, "tell me! Tell me!" I said, "I will, I will! At lunch."

During the entire school day leading up to lunch, I was so excited to share with my friend what had happened the night before that it just could not come fast enough! The bell rang, and off to the cafeteria I jetted. I went right in and found my friend who was already waiting on me. I went through the line to get my lunch, then sat down by Cassandra. I could hardly finish blessing my food before she plunged into saying, "Girl!? What happened?!" I took a bit of my food and then proceeded to tell her exactly what had happened. She asked, "So, what's his name?" And after telling her his name, Cassandra paused with this puzzled-like look on her face.

So, I said, "What??"

She said, "Tell me his name again."

And I did. Cassandra immediately covered her mouth and gasped. "Oh my God," she said.

Now I was confused, and I said, "Tell me! What??!"

She screamed, "I THINK I KNOW HIM!!"

At that moment, my heart began to flutter, my hands began to sweat, and I felt like a nervous wreck. With only a few minutes left for lunch, by this time, my appetite had escaped my entire pallet. Cassandra paused with tears in her eyes, and we both sat still for a moment. Then I asked, "How do you know my father?" She responded by basically saying that the church that she was attending was his family church. My mouth dropped in total disbelief. Before we knew it, the bell rang, and it was time to go back to class. It was good that Cassandra and I shared one more period later in the day because we planned on continuing the conversation then.

CHAPTER 6
Going in Circles

"Order my steps in thy word: and let not any iniquity have dominion over me. Deliver me from the oppression of man: so will I keep thy precepts."

— PSALM 119:133-134

Following the conversation Cassandra and I just had, time had an illusion over me as though it had indefinitely frozen in the very essence of everything revealed. The second to last period of the day was social studies. It was in this class that Cassandra and I shared before ending school. It was extremely tough for me to concentrate on anything since I heard everything illuminated. As time proceeded throughout the class, I was beginning to get relatively anxious and impatient while waiting to go to social studies with Cassandra. My anxiety must have been visibly noticeable at this point because even my teacher came to ask if I was doing okay, and I gave her a nod to let her know I was well.

Finally, the bell rang, and it was time to go to social studies. I darted out of the door to get into the next room. At this moment, I was extremely grateful we didn't have assigned seats, leaving us at liberty to sit where we pleased as long as we did our work. Our teacher would write our assignments for the day on the board. Once Cassandra and I took our seats, we got right to work so we'd have more time to talk. Upon completion of our work, we immediately began talking where we left off.

I had to make sure she was confident it was my father she spoke about knowing.

Cassandra assured me she was almost positive it was. I started asking more questions about her Pastor, and she explained to me how large and talented my father and his family were. What made me most excited was how excited Cassandra was telling me about my father and her church. I asked her when exactly she would ask her Pastor about knowing my father, and she said the next time she attended service. The end of the period had come, and I was far from ready to be done with the conversation we were having. As we parted, she promised me that she was going to get answers for me.

I walked away, completely stunned and overwhelmed at what I had discovered yet again. And the thought of the possibility that I may get the chance to meet my father? For a moment, escape to the mind of a young girl. Imagine her utterly unaware of a broken heart caused by the absence of her biological genetics. See the girl wandering throughout life, being as normal as one could be. But the moment she's enlightened to a piece of her missing, she's led to a road that discovers the unknown. And atlas, you're being faced with the opportunity of that very void filled. That's what I felt at that moment. My imagination was running wild with the wind in time at the places we may go, the things he might say, and the reasons behind his long-lived absence discovered.

Along with all my thoughts concerning reunification with my father, I couldn't help but notice how my desire had never been so strong to meet my actual dad due to my grandfather always being there for me. On the way home, I was thinking about how my father would look. I wondered if he'd be tall or short. Or whether he was skinny or stocky. I mean, after all, it didn't matter much how he looked. Still, I wanted to know all there was to know about my dad.

After finally arriving home, I walked in, and my mother was cooking dinner, as usual. She was such an excellent cook. I always looked forward to dinnertime. But with Mom, one thing's for sure, and two things are for certain; she knew when something was wrong with me or if something was on my mind. She asked me if I was okay, and I responded with, "Yes, ma'am, I'm okay." I had not shared with her or my siblings what all I had learned of my father just yet. So, I stayed silent for the most part and continued to do what was expected of me. I was a well-behaved child, and I rarely got whoopings. Unlike a few of my brothers, they received corrections weekly to behave correctly. When Mom gave instructions out for the household, I always made sure to follow them. I rarely had any trouble with my siblings as it pertains to them listening to me. There wasn't much TV watching for us either, so we learned how to play and get along with each other very well.

Because of this, there was seldom any fighting between all of us siblings.

Gratefully, our home was very peaceful and shockingly quiet, considering all of the children there were in it. I didn't indulge in too many games, but I did enjoy doing hair. I started by just practicing on the half-head Barbie dolls. Then I progressed to doing my sisters' hair regularly. Our allowed agenda mainly was church and school.

Anything outside of that we were hardly a part of. Of course, we could play outside, but that was as far as freedom went. Mom was very protective of us, and she didn't trust many people to care for us. Because of this, my leisure time was full of singing, reading, or babysitting.

By the time night fell, I couldn't force sleep on myself fast enough out of anticipation to get to school and speak to Cassandra the next day. When morning finally came, and I arrived at school, I was more than disappointed to discover Cassandra's absence. My day grew very long without my friend there to tell me all she had possibly learned after our talk the day before. And considering she and I rarely spoke on the phone, the school was our only opportunity for communication. For the rest of that week, Cassandra remained absent from school. Her absence made me start to think that maybe she could not prove all she had promised to discover for me. The thought of this had my mind all over the place and, unfortunately, doubting my friend.

CHAPTER 7
The Journey Begins

As a little girl, I loved going to church. At the end of services, my grandfather would host the alter call. I'd always get in the line so my grandfather could pray for me. He'd ask what I wanted God to do for me, and I'd always say that I just wanted to be better. As much as I loved going to church, this particular weekend could not be over quick enough as I was very much so in great anticipation to get back to school.

I got up earlier than usual that next day, just praying that Cassandra would be at school. Sure enough, once arriving at my second period, there awaited Cassandra. The joy that filled my heart to see her was more incredible than ever before. I ran up to her and gave her the biggest hug. I asked, "Where have you been?!"

She replied, "I'm sorry, I've been sick."

I said, "Oh no! I began to get worried. Did you ever get a chance to talk to your Pastor?"

And right before the bell rang, she told me that she was able to speak to her. My heart began to race faster than a turbo engine in a Maserati Gran Turismo. Of course, we were interrupted by the bell yet again, leaving me on a cliff-hanger. Despite my excitement, I had to remain fair to my friend, knowing she had a lot of work to catch up on due to being sick. At this point, I had no choice but to wait for lunch to discuss all that Cassandra had discovered this time. The anxiety of waiting made me very nervous for the rest of the day.

Before I knew it, the bell rang again, and it was time for lunch. I skipped getting in the line and went right to the table to listen to what Cassandra had to tell me. She started by saying that she had great news for me. She went to her Pastor and let her know that I was looking for my father. With this, Cassandra found out the Pastor of her church just so happened to be my great-aunt, and unbelievably, her nephew was my father. In this conversation, my aunt disclosed to her that my father lived in Toledo, Ohio, and wanted to see me. Wow! At this moment, I didn't know whether to cry, run, scream, or laugh. Cassandra told me my aunt's name. She also said that my aunt remembered my mother due to fellowshipping with our church before. In these short few minutes, my life had changed entirely from not knowing who my father was to discovering he was closer than I had ever thought.

The feelings that I experienced at that moment, I'm sure, mirror any girl discovering her father. After going through what seemed to have been an entire LAPD case of finding a missing person and getting all of this information on a man that I would soon call "Daddy," it all began to get so real. On top of my precious high school friend, Cassandra, this realization turned out to be the very catalyst to the entire case, an impossible feeling this all was.

The severity of this situation had grown to be more than I, as a child, could handle. Throughout the day, I was trying to figure out how to tell my mother about everything revealed to me. I found my emotional barometer to be somewhere in between excitement and worry. Honestly, I didn't know what I was supposed to do or how exactly I should feel. At times, I'd laugh and be tickled with excitement. And at other times, I found myself a little upset and confused. I couldn't help but wonder, with him always being that close, why didn't he ever try to see me?

By this time, the second to last period of this emotionally filled day had finally come, and I was able to talk to my friend. We proceeded to do our work, as usual. Then we picked back up where we left off. I couldn't help but ask her to repeat everything to me, exactly how she said it before. And she did just that. I needed her to say everything slowly, to make sure I fully understood every word. This time, she let me know that my aunt got a little emotional as she began remembering precisely who my family and I were. Cassandra went on to say that my aunt would be calling my father in Toledo to let him know that "his daughter wanted to see him." By this time, I had an ocean of tears in my eyes, and I was doing all that I could do not to start sobbing in Social Studies.

Cassandra paused to make sure I was okay.

I let her know that I was just okay but immensely overwhelmed. She reached into her purse, provided me with some tissues, and asked if I needed a moment alone. In that space, I just wanted her there. She was okay to say nothing else and to be there. I thanked her so much for talking to her Pastor on my behalf and being ever so diligent in helping me find my father. I knew I had found a gem in Cassandra because her only intention for helping me was to be a good friend and be able to help me get everything I ever wanted.

As I entered into the last period of the day, with so much on my mind, my genuine desire was to call it a day and go home. I was ready to stare into space for the rest of the day. At this point, every word that my teacher said went in one ear and out of the other. Now the only thing that filled my mind was how on earth I was going to tell my mother all that I had done and how she would react to knowing. The ride home on the bus seemed to have been way too fast, which let me know that I wasn't ready to get home to my mother just yet. As I started to walk up the doorway, I felt excited and ill at the same time. As usual, Mom greeted me at the door and asked how my day went. I responded by telling her that my day went fine. After speaking to my mother, I went upstairs to my room, I dropped my bags, and I just sat there. My two sisters and I shared a room. One was six years old, and the other was three years old. My two-year-old baby brother stayed in our room for most of the time as well. They were always ready to jump around, talk, and play. On this day, I was not in the mood to do any of those things. The four of us, in particular, were very close. They looked to me as a second parent due to my constant care toward them. Although my mother was married at the time, my step-father and I were not close at all, and I did not call him "Dad." I wasn't a massive fan of him due to how he treated my brothers. He did do an excellent job at taking care of us. Still contemplating when and if I was going to tell my mother about the information that I received. Mind you, an arduous contemplation considering how frozen I felt when Cassandra first said everything to me.

The days ahead were heavily anticipated while waiting to hear if Cassandra got any more concerning my father. I found myself beginning to write his name several times in my notebook daily. In the past, I had several people tell me that I had neat handwriting. I started thinking of the things I would say if I ever got a chance to meet him. I began to wonder what my reaction would be. Would I cry or be assertive? Would I jump into his arms or merely stare? There were so many thoughts that just kept cycling throughout my mind nonstop. I wondered if he had any other children. Was he married? Was he rich? I constantly prayed that my father would desire to know and spoil me. A few weeks had passed at this point, and I still hadn't heard anything concerning my father. Then all of a sudden, Cassandra handed me a note that said that my father was coming into town in a few weeks and that he wanted to see me. He wanted to see *me*.

CHAPTER 8
Waiting for the Call

J ust pause for a second. Just please, slow the pace of time down for my thirteen-year-old, overwhelmed, fast-beating heart for just five minutes. My emotions were very oxymoron-ish, which I know, "Oxymoron-ish" is not a word. But at this moment, my feelings were so contradicting. I wanted time to pause just so that I could breathe, but I also wanted time to just fast forward to the part where I could see him. Where I could put an end to all of this anxiety and uncertainty about what I felt was real but I could not presently see or feel. Cassandra said that *my* father wanted to see *me*. Me?!

Lunchtime could not be here quick enough for Cassandra to repeat in words to me that she had written on that note. My heart pulsated at a tempo so loud and fast that I'm pretty sure my fellow students could hear it as I walked swiftly to get to my friend. I proceeded to sit down at the table, and Cassandra began speaking immediately. She spoke with such excitement and passion in her voice. She asked, "Are you ready to see your father?" And I just sat there staring at her. As I tried to obtain any audible answer from her, the only thing that I could muster up was a head nod. I felt paralyzed with excitement and fear at this point. I went to try and open my carton of milk, and my shaky hands wouldn't even allow it. Cassandra took the carton and opened it for me. She began explaining that there was some kind of musical that was to take place at her church and that my father had planned on attending. She then said that he wanted to speak to me on the phone. I let her know that I was now going to have to tell my mother about it all because I wouldn't be able to give my number out to anyone without asking permission from her. I knew that I wasn't going to be able to keep this from my mom, but receiving this information had now forced me to tell her whether I was ready or not.

My nerves were now getting to me pretty heavily for the remainder of the school day. I had to decide whether I was going to lie to my mom and say that Cassandra made me find him or whether I'd just tell her the plain truth. I just began to think about the possibility of hurting my mother's feelings by going behind her back with all of this and the possible trouble I could get into because of it. As the school bus stopped at my destination, I jumped off, running to my house so fast, to the point I nearly knocked my mother over at the door from trying to get upstairs to my room. Once getting into my room, I took the longest inhale in an attempt to try and gain control over my anxiety. Then finally, I decided it was time to tell my mother all that I had been keeping from her. I went downstairs, and she was preparing for dinner as usual. So, I sat down at the table, and I said, *"Mom... I'd like to talk to you about something that has been on my mind."*

She responded by saying, *"Okay, go ahead."*

I said, *"Do you remember when I asked you about my father?"*

She replied, *"Yes."*

I continued to tell her that I had a friend at school who began to share with me about her life. My mother continued cooking as I proceeded with the conversation. I let her know that the dialogue between Cassandra and I grew to talking about our parents, and in that vein, Cassandra asked me what my father's name was. Mom was still very quiet. I went on to explain that once I told her my father's name, she had revealed that her Pastor was my father's aunt. By this time, my mother had begun washing her hands and slowly turned around to face me. That really made me nervous about what she may have done or said at this point. But she remained quiet. I went on to tell her that my father's aunt called him in Toledo, Ohio, and because of this, he wanted to come to Columbus to see me. After me saying all of this, there was complete silence for what felt like forever, but in reality, it was only about five seconds. Finally breaking her silence, she asked, "When is he supposed to be coming?" I let her know that he was set to arrive in a few weeks.

Mom had a look on her face that was somewhere in between disgust and hurt. But still, she asked me what *I* wanted to do. Very nervously, I replied, "I want to meet my father." My mother sighed and gave me the consent that it would be okay if I was to meet my dad.

Needless to say, I almost choked on my own spit due to my mom hardly ever giving me answers right away about anything. I thanked her so much and said that I'd find out exactly when he was to arrive in town. After getting all of that out, I had just one more request, and that was to allow him to call the house phone to speak to me. I knew that I was pushing it at this point, but I thought that I should just go ahead and try my luck. She sighed again and nodded reluctantly. By the time we finished the conversation, I was skipping and humming as I ran up the stair to my room. My siblings were very curious as to why I was so happy all of a sudden. I let them know that I would tell them later. It was so hard to sleep throughout this night out of anticipation of getting to school the next day and telling Cassandra the good news.

Up early the following morning, I made haste in cleaning my room and getting dressed in order to get to school as quickly as possible. While I remember the weather, this day being gloomy; I also remember being on a cloud so high that not even drugs could emulate the same feeling that I felt at this moment. My heart was so overjoyed just knowing that I would *finally* be fortunate enough to meet my father in a few weeks.

Second period finally came, Cassandra arrived, and within a matter of a minute, I had told her everything my mother had said to me the night before. My friend was just as happy as I was about all of the news. Following this conversation, she gave me her Pastor's number. By this time, we both were so filled with excitement that we began to giggle at everything. This was definitely not in the norm for my personality. Even with all of our excitement, we still had to maintain a level of poise and discipline in order to get all of the work done for that period.

As the day proceeded to pass, I found myself writing down my father's name repeatedly in my journals. How consumed I remember being at just the mere thought of meeting my father, anticipating and imagining what he might have looked like, and wondering if I at all resembled him as well. My mind wandered in the unknown for hours, trying to simply beat the future to what reality could have looked like when it actually happened. My mind lived in this space daily while waiting.

A week had now gone by, and my excitement was only growing by the hour. As time drew closer, I couldn't help but notice my mother's silence growing quieter and quieter. I believe her silence was due to her praying because that's what it would normally mean in the past. Every time that phone rang, my heart would skip two beats, just hoping that it was my father. That Thursday evening, my mother called me from upstairs, saying there was someone on the phone who would like to speak to me. At this point, I just presumed it to be one of my church friends or cousins. I came down as she asked, grabbed the phone, and said, *"Hello?"*

A man's voice replied, *"Hi baby, this is your daddy."* Finally, the moment had come. It was *him;* it was my father. I had to have been frozen for at least three seconds.

Finally, I mustered up enough courage to say hello back with a huge smile on my face. My mother must have known that it was him because she remained standing there the entire duration that my father and I spoke. But she didn't *just* stand there. She stood there with this glare that managed to pierce me from the outside in. However, I couldn't let the fear of her death-stare stop me from relishing in the moment of hearing the one voice that I had been yearning after for weeks. My father asked me how I was doing, that he loved me, and that he'd always wanted to be in my life. He then asked my mother if he could take me out to eat when he came to town. I looked over at my mother for confirmation or denial, and she reluctantly nodded her head at me, saying yes to his request. Lord, did my heart dive deep into the happiest of seas that had ever existed. My father assured me that he would answer all of my questions upon arriving in a few weeks. He and I stayed on the phone for about ten minutes. He told me once again that he loved me, and I told him the same.

After hanging up the phone, I took off sprinting to my room with the biggest smile tattooed on my face. I know that my smile was more than noticeable because my siblings wouldn't stop asking me what the grin was for. My feeling of undeniable excitement was just too good not to share. I told them that I had spoken to my father for the first time. Out of the seven of us, before then, my two youngest siblings were the only ones who knew of their father because my mother was married to him. As for the other five of us, we all had different fathers, and they did not share the same privilege of knowing their fathers until they reached adulthood. With this, I do believe that my excitement at the time prevented me from using proper judgment in my sharing to consider that my siblings, who did not know their father, may feel a little jealous.

However, I was overall grateful to know they still shared excitement for me.

CHAPTER 9
I Look Just Like Him

I t was with immense anticipation that I felt while looking forward to the days ahead that would lead me to meet the other half of my biological contributor face-to-face finally. I continued writing his name down in my generals over and over again every day at school. Cassandra continuously acted as my haven to share every emotion I had leading up to the big day. My mind constantly moved with curiosity about how I would behave when it was time to meet him. I got lost in a forest of emotions about what I would feel, what I would say to him and how I would say it.

Within the two-week time frame, my father called me again to share with me a little more about him before his arrival. He let me know that he was married to a Caucasian woman and a Bishop in his uncle's organization. My father being is a Bishop? My father, a BISHOP?! The joy I felt looking up to my grandfather, a Bishop, knowing my father was one too. Although I'm pretty sure at that point, it brought me joy to hear my father say just about anything to me. The tone of his voice, the calming that I felt when he called me *"his baby."* Who would have ever imagined that I would find *my* father through my best friend in high school? And here I was, dreading high school!

Each day began to seem like a newborn, discovering that I had ten fingers and the same for toes. It felt as though I had just found that when the sun rose, it created day and that when the moon was exposed, it was to be called night. That I had just discovered that I not only had a mother but that I had this man who also played a role in creating me, and that was my father.

I still wasn't quite sure of how my mother felt because she remained quiet.

Anytime I'd mention anything about my father, she would reply with, "That's nice." Her response was admittedly a little difficult for me to deal with, but I couldn't let that dissuade me from soaking up every emotion of excitement that I had leading up to seeing my daddy. Every time I would go to church, I just began praising God that he had gifted me to connect to my father. Oh, and I had more than enough chances to give my praises. I mean, there were plenty of revivals, quartet concerts, choir rehearsals, and just plain Ol' church being had for me to do so.

Thursday. That was the day. Thursday arrived so swiftly that it almost felt like forever. I could hardly function in any of my classes in school from being so distracted by what was to come when I got back home. Once I got off the bus, I ran home so quickly and started to get dressed immediately. My little brothers and sisters began to cry because they wanted to get dressed too. I admit, I spoiled them bad. Everywhere I went, there they followed. So, they were a bit bent out of shape, knowing they couldn't come. To provide some comfort to their little hearts, I dressed them too.

"Tic-Tok" went the clock. I was all dressed and patiently yet, eagerly awaiting my father's arrival while sitting on the front porch. I skipped eating dinner at home because my daddy was taking me out to eat. Plus, there was no way I'd risk getting my outfit dirty. During one of our previous conversations, my dad told me that he would be arriving in a small, black truck. There I was, more anxious and excited than I think my body had ever felt. I sat and watched every car that came down 17th Avenue by the bridge leading to the fairgrounds. About thirty minutes had passed, then suddenly, there it was; a black truck driving slowly down the road toward me. My heart began to beat so fast as I stared. In a split second, time had suddenly frozen as he and my eyes locked. A smile that took over his entire face appeared, and I thought I was going to faint instantly from excitement. I felt like I was looking in the mirror because I looked just like him.

The truck that Dad drove had one bench in it, enough for three people only. While he was driving up, I could see another person in the front seat with him. When the vehicle slowed down, he asked, "Are you, Sylvia?"

"Yes, sir," I responded, and he began to park. By then, I spoke to my mother through the screen door and let her know that my father had arrived, and she came outside. As he proceeded to get out of the truck, I noticed that he was a stocky-looking man. He stood at about 5'8 and had black hair and bow legs. It was almost like I became mesmerized and numb at the same time at this moment. I remember feeling like I was in some dream that was far too good to be true. Thursday had officially become the best day of my life. And that if it was a dream, I didn't want to wake up anytime soon! I now knew what it felt like to be that little girl waiting for her estranged father to show up and how it felt for me to be the apple of his eye.

As I snapped back into reality, I realized that I was still sitting on the porch, just staring. I finally got the strength to stand and prepare to leave. My siblings stood right beside me, waiting for him to approach me on the porch. The lady that was with him stayed in the car as he came to speak. When he came to me, he said hello to my mother first, and then my mother introduced me to him. My father reached out his arms to embrace me, and I could've dropped to the ground right there. I felt like I was floating in heaven. Ironically, my father asked if my siblings were my children, and I clarified them. My father then asked my mother if it was okay to take me to get something to eat, and she again said yes. As we began to leave, my siblings started to cry because they wanted to come with me. I reassured them that I would be back, although it seemed to help very little. As we walked down the stairs, my father held my hand and kept telling me how beautiful I was.

I kept thanking him while shaking out of excitement and nervousness to the car. The walk was relatively short but seemed so very long. When approaching the truck, he opened the door for me to get in, and the lady sitting inside got out as I got in. I slid over to the middle, and the lady returned to the truck. Once my father got into the vehicle on the driver's side, we pulled off, and he introduced the lady to me and me. We exchanged a "hello" following the introduction. My father must have sensed that I was nervous because he gently held my hand while driving.

I had the slightest of clues as to where we were going, but it didn't matter at all because I felt safe with my father, and I trusted that wherever we went, I'd be just fine. We pulled up to this house, and when we got there, he told the lady that he would pick her up later. She exited the truck, and we drove away. There was a bit of small talk exchanged between him and me during this ride. There were also lots of smiles, and the phrase "I love you" was often exchanged. After riding around for a little, my father asked me what I wanted to eat. I told him that a hamburger would be fine. We then stopped, and he got me a burger. We went to the park and sat in the parking lot while I ate. My father did most of the talking, asking me a few questions in between. He began telling me how he and my mother met years ago and that he was at least seven years older than my mother at the time. He said he didn't know that Mother had conceived until after I was born. He also mentioned that he tried to visit but that my grandfather prohibited him from seeing me and that his assistance was unnecessary in raising me. I asked him if he had ever thought about me in the last fifteen years, and he assured me that there wasn't a day that went by that he did not think of me. Dad even said that he would cry some nights because he had twenty-two children by various women, and he could not see me. Wow! Was I astonished to hear everything that he had shared?! I made sure to soak up every word that he spoke to me.

My father had shared so much in so little time, and all of it was pretty overwhelming. However, he wasn't done sharing just yet. Dad said that although he was a religious man, he did believe that it was okay to drink. He said that he considered himself to be like King David from the Bible. I asked him what he meant by saying that. My father told me that he had several concubines (a lot of wives simultaneously.) As one could imagine, as a fifteen-year-old, I had never heard of that before, but I knew it could not have been Godly. Even with this in mind, I had to remind myself that no one was perfect and that I had to restrain myself from judging my father but pray for him. He was my father, and nothing was going to change that for me.

My father wanted to know more about me and the things that I enjoyed doing. I told him that I love God, church, enjoy school, singing, playing the keyboard, and love my family. My father said that he was a musician. Dad directed choirs, sang, played the keyboard, and enjoyed making things. Hearing all that he did was so exciting to hear from my father as it let me know that I had inherited my musical abilities from him. After getting to know each other a little more, Dad kept asking me if I was okay. After a while, he began to cry and kept hugging me while telling me he loved me and how much he missed me. At this point, I didn't know how to respond. However, I hugged him and told him that I loved him too. In my mind, I'm not sure what I expected out of meeting my father, but I don't think I expected him to be like this. He told me that he never imagined that I would look the way that I did. He asked me if I had always looked older than I was, and I told him that I did.

The hour had continued growing late, and it was time for me to return home. My father assured me that he would always protect me and ensure that no one would harm me. He continued holding my hand until we arrived in front of my home on the way back

home. He turned the truck off and pulled me close to him once again. He told me how much he loved me and that he was not ready to leave me. Just before it was time for me to get out of the truck, he held my face and began to kiss my forehead, then my cheek, and then he kissed me in the mouth. I was overtaken with excitement this entire time while being with my father, but I was a little confused at this moment. Remembering the words that he had just spoken to me, I held on to my father's arm, trusting that despite how I felt, he would not let anything happen to me. I proceeded to get out of the truck as he opened the door for me. He walked me up the stairs to my house and promised that he would be back to see me again in two weeks.

CHAPTER 10

My Daddy

And just like that, existing at this time was a fifteen-year-old little girl who slept, ate, and drank all things, *Daddy*. That term never actually came out of my mouth just yet, but several times in my head. I couldn't wait to get to school to tell Cassandra about my first outing with my father. I felt as if my whole world had shifted entirely and that life was taking a swift turn for the better. When arriving at school, Cassandra was too excited for me and wanted to hear every detail from the beginning until the end. She kept saying that my eyes were dancing while talking about my daddy. I told her that he was coming back in a few weeks and could hardly contain my excitement. That Saturday morning, my mother and I worked together preparing breakfast. While doing so, she asked me how my visit with my father was. I made sure to stay modest and only show subtle excitement while telling her about his time. In doing so, I was trying not to make her feel bad by showing too much excitement. Besides, it was a little difficult even to show too much emotion because my mother kept the same look on her face the entire time while talking. However, I continued to tell her about some of the things that my dad shared with me. I knew if I told her about everything that my daddy shared, she'd end all contact with him immediately.

By the time I almost finished sharing, the rest of my siblings had come downstairs for breakfast. I continued setting the table and prepared the plates for each child. It was very enlightening that my father had asked if my siblings were my children. I mean, I had been used to the routine of being their secondary caretaker. Don't get me wrong; I loved my siblings. However, at times, it became so frustrating and overwhelming to watch time drift away. It felt like as time passed, so did my childhood.

Nevertheless, I made sure that my siblings were cared for; and if there was ever a time that I didn't feel up to it, they made sure that I did anyway. My family and I would get talked about often in the church world. As a result of this, I naturally became very overprotective of my siblings. They'd always gossip about my mother and the number of children she had. While doing so, they had no idea that we could hear what they'd say. It affected me in ways that made me tough and resilient for my family, for my siblings. I had so many feelings about what they would say about us, but I knew not to say anything that would take me out of a "child's place." So, I just continued expressing myself through speaking by way of music. Of course, there came a time when boys and men would attempt to grab my attention as well, but the only thing on my mind was my daddy and how lucky I considered myself to have him in my world.

We approached the middle of fall, and it was almost time for mom to call Charity Newsies to come and check out our clothes. I was not too fond of this process, and I dreaded that knock on our door. I said to myself that I was going to ask my Daddy to buy me new clothes just so that I could avoid wearing those worn-down Charity Newsies items. As days drew closer, I anticipated my Daddy calling me more and more. The anticipation became so intense that my heart would skip a beat at the phone's ringing.

However, every time it would be my cousins or church friends. I knew that I was over everything except for my daddy.

When I would talk to anyone other than him, I had very little to say. I could sense that I was starting to get somewhat irritated a lot more at my siblings, stepfather, and some of the things my mother would say and do. I worked hard every day to sense the attitude because my mother would have some things to say about that. Continuing to do what was expected of me, inwardly, I wondered how my daddy would feel about me moving in with him. Honestly, I was shocked at myself that I would even think of such a thing. My mother and my siblings were all that I knew. However, after my first meeting with my daddy, I had my mind set; I wanted to be around my daddy forever. I made sure to note it in my mind to tell him about my request when he came back to see me.

Two days before his arrival, my daddy called and said that he would be in Columbus soon. He told me to ask mom again if he could pick me up once he arrived. I asked, and mom said yes. My Daddy began to ask me what I had been doing since we last saw each other. I'm pretty sure that I did more giggling than talking when he'd ask me questions. After all the giggles died down, Daddy asked me if I felt any different about him after hearing some of the information he shared the first time we met. I told him that my feelings did not change and that I'd continue praying for him. After saying this, he chuckled a little and said he would see me in a few days. He told me that he "loved me," and I returned the phrase to him as we hung up the phone. To hear those words from Daddy was priceless, and they continued to ring in my ear for the rest of the evening. Again, I went dancing up the stairs straight into my room and lay across the bed, wondering what I was to wear when he came this time.

Saturday came, and I was happy because I'd get to stay out a little longer. After all, it wasn't a school night. I woke nearly five hours earlier than time to get ready for my day with Daddy. I took a bath and expeditiously got dressed and ready to go. To be expected, my siblings hovered around, wanting to go with me again. My mother let them know that it was my day to spend with my daddy. About three hours later, a knock came at the door, and it was Daddy. Mom called me down to the stairs, and I darted down as quickly as I could. When I came down, I reached out and kissed him on the cheek. He asked me if I was ready to go, and I let him know that I was. Mom carried a heavy sadness on her face as she waved bye to me, and I told her that I loved her. We got into the truck, just him and I, and we pulled off. Daddy asked me if I wanted to sit beside him, and I slid over to the driver's side without hesitation. He asked, "How's my baby today?"

I responded, "Great, Daddy." Yes, I said the name out loud finally, Daddy.

He put his arms around me with a big smile and told me how much he loved me. He shared that ever since the time he left me last, he had not been able to think about anyone else except for me. He asked me where I wanted to eat this time, and I told him that White Castle's would be fine. So, we pulled into the drive-thru, received our order, and sat in the parking lot as we ate. Daddy didn't eat much, but he did watch me the entire time. He smiled as he continuously touched my face gently. He began asking me a series of questions again. My daddy asked if I had a boyfriend- I informed him that I did not at that time. Then he asked if I was a virgin, drowning in shame; I told him that I was not a virgin. He then asked how many men had I slept with, and I told him that I only had one. Daddy lifted my head and reassured me that I did not have to be ashamed anymore because he would not let anyone else "abuse" me. I looked at him and smiled slightly, and then he reached over and began to kiss me in the mouth once again. I quickly pulled away in shock, and he began to apologize and said that I was just so beautiful. He said that he was just overly excited to have found me after all of these years.

Daddy had begun to cry at this point. I noticed this brown paper bag that had some drink in it. The glass smelled a little different, but I thought that maybe it was cologne. I remembered him telling me that he drank for pleasure, but I shied away from asking him what was in the bag. I couldn't understand why Daddy was crying, so I asked him. He said that he was crying out of fear of losing me. I reassured him that would never happen. Following this, we began to drive again. When the truck stopped, I noticed that we were at a bar. Before I could even utter a word, he told me that he wanted to introduce me to some of his friends. I'm sure he could tell that I was nervous. He reassured me that he wouldn't let anything happen to me and that I could trust him because he was my daddy. I went along with it, although I was still really shaken up. Daddy opened the car door and took me by the hand as he let me into the bar. As we walked in, I kept inwardly praying for God's protection because I had never been in anything like this before. There were so many older men and women that it surprised me, seeing as it was still daytime. While there at the bar, he never let go of my hand as he introduced me to all his friends. They all began to tell me how pretty they felt I was. I didn't know what to do except to stay as close as possible to my daddy. We stood at the bar for a few minutes while Daddy ordered a drink for him and a soda for me before sitting down at a table. There were holes in the walls, and the smell of smoke filled the air. The place felt so dirty to me. The entire atmosphere of this place was so foreign to me. Daddy just kept reminding me to relax. I was getting a little antsy and was quite frankly ready to leave. I asked him how long we would be there, and he told me about fifteen more minutes until he'd take me home.

Ironically, while sitting at the table, he asked me if I wanted to come and live with him someday. Despite everything that had happened until now, my heart remained stuck on everything *Daddy*. I happily told him that I would love to move with him. He smiled while reaching his hand over the table to hold mine while saying that "he'd love that too." He asked me if I was still scared to be in the bar, and I nodded yes. He responded by telling me to gather my things so that we could go. I was so relieved to be going back to breathable air again finally. Once getting back into the truck, Daddy took some spray and sprayed it on me to get rid of the smoke smell. We stayed in the parking lot for around thirty more minutes talking. He kept telling me how beautiful I was and how he didn't expect me to look the way I did. I just sat there listening. He pulled me closer to him again and kissed me in the mouth. Only this time, he used his tongue. I pulled away once again and looked at him, slightly puzzled, and at the same time, I continued to try my best to brush it off and blame it on how happy we were to see each other at the time finally. I just kept reminding myself that this emotion would wear off eventually. Plus, I figured that he was just drunk and was not fully aware of what he was doing.

Daddy continued to hold my hand as he sobbed most of the way home while constantly telling me that he was sorry. Dad said he loved me and that he didn't want to scare me away. I told him that everything was going to be alright because I was going to pray for him. Once arriving back at my home, he opened the truck door and said good night to me and that he would call me in a few days. I kissed him on the cheek, told him that I loved him, and went inside my home. Once I got inside, my mother asked me how my evening had gone. I just responded with "fine" and made my way up to my room. My siblings were playing, but they stopped to say hello to me before I entered my room. I could tell they had just eaten because I could smell the food on their breath. My middle sister asked me what I ate, and I told her hamburgers and fries. Of course, she wondered where hers was, and I just looked at her with a smirk on my face. The little ones jumped up on the bed with me and climbed on my back while I lay across the bed. Although they got on my nerves at the time, I loved them so much. In some way, having them there with me at that moment was comforting. While lying there, I couldn't help but think about everything that had transpired that evening. In my heart, I knew that most of that evening went wrong. However, I was still trying to reason with myself about why he did what he did. I kept convincing myself that it would get better. I mean, it had to. After all, he was my daddy. I kept reminding myself of what the Bible told us, "For all have sinned, and come short of the Glory of God." (Romans 3:23) So, I did what I felt like any Christian should do, and I counted this to be his shortcoming. No matter how many flaws my daddy had, I still wanted to be a part of his life. Nothing else was more evident to me that God had put us together in this moment so that I could pray him through his weaknesses for him to be an excellent Bishop like my grandfather. Considering it all, I made a promise to myself to keep what I knew about my daddy between The Lord and me. The only thing that was on my mind now was moving in with Daddy and how spoiled I would be when I did.

Since I helped my mother so much with taking care of my siblings, I figured that it was time for me to be taken care of by my daddy. As the days continued to pass by, the desire to leave what I had always known grew stronger and stronger. I loved my mother tremendously, but I was ready for change. The only challenge I faced at this moment was how I was going to deliver my request to my mother about possibly moving in with my daddy. My mother depended on me so greatly, and with this news, I knew it would be far from easy.

CHAPTER 11
Meeting the Family

On a day proceeding our last time seeing one another, daddy called me saying that his family church was to have a significant function and that he'd like to pick me up after our services to introduce me to the family. I was so happy to hear him speak of God and church, considering all that had taken place up until this point. He said that there were several preachers, singers, and musicians in the family that I would be able to meet. This time, I let daddy ask my mother himself if I could attend the family event. My mother said that I could go. I was slightly anxious to meet the rest of the family. During this time, there was church all day long. There would be Sunday school at 9:30 am, morning worship at 11:00 am, afternoon service at 3:00 pm, Young People's Love Joy Band at 6:00 pm, and Radio Broadcast at 7:00 pm. Being that I'd be going with my daddy, that would mean that I was to miss most of the regular services on that particular Sunday.

The Sunday had finally arrived. Daddy picked me up from my church, and then we went over to his cousin's church, where everyone else was to gather at 6:00 pm. Once arriving at my father's cousin's church, there were cars everywhere. There was even a limousine parked in the front of the building. Daddy let me know that it was asked of me to sing that day. I was excited to participate in this service, mainly because he had never heard me sing before. Before service started, Daddy introduced me to anyone that would listen. He was so proud to tell everyone who I was. Everyone kept telling me how pretty I was and that I looked just like my father. Many of my cousins could not believe that I was only fifteen. Daddy had his wife and two kids with him. His wife appeared to be nice, but she didn't have a lot to say. It was so neat to see him in a suit seeing that he had only been in casual attire when seeing him in the past.

Service had finally begun. Daddy was instructed to get on the piano, and he started singing too. Daddy played and sang so well. It was amazing to see that pretty much everyone in the building had some musical talent. The remainder of the service entailed music, singing, and praises that lasted all evening. It had come time for me to sing. When walking up to the alter, nerves completely took over as all eyes were on me. I sang my song and was under the impression that I had finished. I'd venture to say I did a pretty good job seeing as though the audience wouldn't let me go to my seat without singing another song. This time, Daddy came and sang with me. That made the audience cheer and shout. The love and joy that I felt with an evening surrounded by my new family felt terrific. After service, there was a reception held in the fellowship hall. We all took pictures and exchanged phone numbers with my family and me.

It was now time for me to return home after all of the festivities of the day. We said our goodbyes, and Daddy proceeded to take me home. On the way, I finally got the chance to talk a little more to his wife and my two brothers, which I thoroughly enjoyed. They even discussed the possibility of me going to Toledo to live and said it would be a pleasure to have me. Boy! Was this music to my ears! To hear his wife be accepting of me living in her home was excellent and very reassuring. My daddy's wife amazed me two times that night. First, to hear her welcome me into her home, and another once hearing that she could sing like a true Sista. By the time our conversation had ended, we had arrived back at my house. I said my goodbyes to everyone and headed inside. Before entering my home, Daddy walked me up the stairs, kissed my cheek, and wished me a good night. I asked if it would be okay if I called him. He instructed me to wait and allow him to call me so that my mother wouldn't have to pay the bill. I told him that I enjoyed myself and that I couldn't wait to see him again. My stepfather let me in this time. However, he didn't have too much to say to my daddy or me.

My Sunday had been full of joy, and I took a lot of time once arriving home to reflect on the events of the day. There was so much to fill Cassandra in on the next day at school. She was supposed to be at the service, but she was unable to attend. The next day, I told Cassandra about the many Cherokee Indians on my daddy's side. She asked if I had informed my mother about my desire to live with my daddy. I let her know that I hadn't gotten around to it quite yet. I was still trying to figure out exactly how to speak to my mother about my relocation request.

Three weeks had passed by, and I had been talking to both my daddy and his wife. Daddy was scheduled to come back into town; however, my mother did not permit me to spend time with him this time. I swore that I must have heard my mother wrong when she denied me visiting him. But she held to her answer with zero hesitation. Her denial of me seeing Daddy provoked an attitude from me immediately. I pouted around the house as if my world had come to an end. Mom looked at me and said, "You better get yourself together, Sylvia LynnAnn!" I rolled my eyes slightly and partially agreed while heading to my room. I could sense that my mother was beginning to draw back from allowing me to see my daddy consistently. Her behavior was when I knew it was time to make my request known to her about relocating.

The next day at school, I told Cassandra that I was planning to run away from home to live with my daddy. She asked me how I was planning on doing such a thing. I told her that I hadn't quite gotten that far just yet. Looking at me with total shock and concern, Cassandra asked, "What prompted this, Sylvia?" I told her that I felt like my mother was fixing to stop me from seeing Daddy. She listened, but she told me to make sure that I prayed about it before making a final decision. I let her know that I would do just that. In my heart, I felt like God had given me the okay to leave by allowing me to find my daddy through a schoolmate. I wanted to be living with my daddy by Christmas time. As I continued to contemplate the plan of running away in my mind, I became even more convinced that I must act fast.

A few weeks went by, and I was beginning to put together my plan to run. I became so consumed by this next move that the secret of it all became overwhelming. So, I decided to share my plan with one of my brothers, who was knowingly quiet. I figured he didn't care anyway, so I told him everything. I planned to pack my bags one afternoon, then act like I would take the trash to the dumpster. The dumpster was in the back of our home across the alley. But instead of taking the garbage out, the "trash" would be my belongings, and my daddy would be waiting there for me. When seeing my daddy, I'd hop in the car and would be gone. My brother continued to read his encyclopedia as if he wasn't paying me much attention. When I finished telling him, I went to my room, set my alarm, and went to bed.

As the morning approached, my mother yelled from downstairs, telling me to immediately get up and come to her. I jumped out of bed, put my slippers on, and started down the stairs. Before even making it down, my mother said, "So, I hear that you are planning to run away, huh?" I stood there frozen, in total shock because this meant that my brother had told her what I said to him. My mother proceeded to say that she could not sleep all night because of what I had said to my brother. She asked me if it was true, and I had no choice but to confirm that it was. My mother asked how long my father and I had planned this, and I told her about a month. The expression that she held on her face; I could never forget. It was as if I'd slapped her. So, Mom told me that if I was willing to take such drastic measures to run away to my father, she'd instead just let me go. At this moment, I just knew I was still sleeping and that the entire morning had been a dream. Only, it wasn't. I was awake, and this was real. I never expected her to give in so quickly or at all. A few seconds of stillness had passed before I headed back up to my room. At first, I wanted to be upset with my brother. But then, I realized he only told because he loved and cared about my well-being. Plus, him telling saved me the trouble of having to tell her myself.

I proceeded to get ready for school and went to catch the bus. While heading to the bus stop, my mind continued to replay what happened that morning. My emotions concerning what happened were intensely conflicted. I didn't know whether to laugh, cry, or scream. Soon after arriving at school, I quickly found Cassandra and told her what had happened that morning. She had great disbelief toward what I said to her. Cassandra wanted to know every detail. We were both late getting to our first-class period that morning.

School couldn't have been over fast enough. My focus was far from the English language and math. That day, I consistently thanked God and Cassandra for helping me find my daddy. Even after all of our conversations, the only true thing on my mind was leaving.

When arriving home, my mother sat on the phone talking to my grandmother. She explained to her what I desired to do. About five minutes later, Mom called me into the living room and handed me the telephone. I said hello, and my grandmother proceeded to tell me what she had heard. Then she said that my grandfather had a message for me. He wanted me to know that if I chose to go to Toledo with my father, I would go through hell before I returned home. I did listen, and when she finished speaking, I told her I understood before giving my mother the phone. Deep down, I knew my family would not take me leaving lightly. So, my grandma and grandpa's reaction did not come as a surprise. Despite what any of them thought, my mind remained set on leaving Columbus, Ohio.

About an hour went by before Daddy called. I was scared that my mother wouldn't let me talk to him, but she did. When I told him that Mom permitted me to move with him, he was shocked and happy at the same time. Mom asked to speak to him, and I gave her the phone and waited. She asked him when he was coming to get me, and he said the following Saturday.

CHAPTER 12
My Good-byes

For the next eight days, I had to break the news to my cousins, church family, and friends of my moving with Daddy. Telling my siblings was by far the most complicated task. After all, I did love them as my own and knew that I'd miss them greatly. Following my siblings, I told the rest of my family, and they grew very sad about my near transition. Through repeatedly telling everyone, I must admit I grew pretty nervous. However, along with those nerves lived great excitement for the new life that awaited me.

Me telling my family the news held no intention of being understood. I knew that most people's opinions on why I should stay came from selfish gain. Ultimately, my brother snitching on my plan to run away became a good thing for me. Instead of my silly plan to throw all of my things away to meet Daddy at the garbage behind the house, I was able to go through my belongings and take my time packing.

With every day that grew closer to my leaving, my mother's face became more broken. The conversations held between us remained were little to none. By this time, strangely, my grandparents' words about my leaving began to replay constantly in my mind. To remain positive, I had to shake it off and remind myself that everything would be alright. I must say, spending time with my siblings grew harder by the day. The thought of no longer seeing them as often started to weigh on me. I knew they couldn't understand fully, and it hurt to see them so broken. To no surprise, Cassandra seemed to be the only one that understood my leaving. She made it so easy to express my feelings to her, and it felt good to be heard and supported by *my* friend.

Through packing, I started to realize how much unnecessary junk I possessed. Mom would peek into my room briefly every day only to see what was going on, and then she'd return downstairs. Honestly speaking, it tore me apart to see my mother so sad. She depended on me for everything, and without me here, she'd have to plan accordingly. I gained peace by knowing after a while, she would adjust, and she would be okay without me. Still, I know my moving hit her with a lot of steam from our family members. I could hear them questioning her on the phone, asking why she allowed my father to take me away from her. Her only response would be that she could only continue praying for me. Mother's response concerning prayer was her default answer the majority of the time.

By the end of the week, time began to speed up drastically. My excitement grew so great that it became hard for me to sleep through the night! When going to school, I held little interest in doing my work. My mind stayed stuck on one thing, moving. My teachers were more than sad to hear I would be living with my father and leaving the school. I'm sure I was one of their favorites. Still, they wished me good luck and hoped things would turn out the way I dreamed. Many guys at the school began asking me if I was actually leaving to move with my dad. When I confirmed it to be accurate, then they'd tell me they had always been interested in me but too scared to say. Them expressing interest at the last moment entertained me none. There was nothing or no one big or shiny enough to get me to stay in Columbus. I remained determined to make this new life work for me.

Thursday evening arrived, and like clockwork, Daddy called to make sure the move was set to play out as planned. Hearing his voice made me even more excited! I asked Daddy what time he'd be arriving in town Saturday, and he let me know he'd be picking me up at 2:00 pm sharp!

Boy, was my heart racing one hundred miles per hour! Daddy's constant giggling let me know he could hear my excitement through the phone.

The day before my leaving, there was "Joy Night Service" held Friday evening. Friday night service turned into a farewell service for my friends and family to say their goodbyes and to corporately pray for my safety while gone. By the time church concluded, there were a few tears shed from all of us. I didn't want anyone thinking I would potentially change my mind, so I tried my best to remain strong. In trying to do so, the facts of how much I'd miss my family remained. When driving home, my siblings, especially the little ones, stayed close to me the entire ride. Once arriving home, they refused to sleep in their beds, knowing it would be my last night with them. So, we stayed up and played games. I started to give them different little things to continue remembering me by. We tried our hardest to stay up all night. However, their little eyes became so heavy that we all just cuddled up together one last time and fell asleep.

The morning seemed to have come quicker than usual. Mom had breakfast prepared for the whole family. We all jumped out of bed, cleaned our rooms, and gathered to eat together for the last time. Everyone remained quiet during breakfast except for the little ones. It was almost like they competed to see who could speak the most within a short time. I knew that they were nervous and sad. However, they tried making the best out of our little time, especially my middle brother. He'd constantly try and make us laugh when he sensed that something was wrong. When we finished eating, we all chipped in with cleaning the kitchen before going upstairs.

By then, it was time for me to bathe and get dressed to be ready when Daddy arrived. I allowed the little ones to follow me around and help me put last-minute items in my suitcases and bags. When I was fully dressed, my siblings sat on my bed, and I told them how much I loved them. I wanted them to know that I'd be sending gifts and visiting them as often as I could. In between each word, I'd kiss their little faces as tears streamed down their cheeks. I reassured them we'd talk to each other at least once a week.

The time had come for me to begin taking my belongings to the door. The bigger boys assisted me with bringing my luggage downstairs. I thanked them for being so strong and not dropping everything all over the floor. I looked at the clock, and it was already 1:45 pm, which meant in fifteen minutes, Daddy would be here, ready to take me to my new life. It was far too cold to wait outside. So, we all stayed in the kitchen, which was near the front door. My mother came out of her room and asked if I had everything I needed. I let her know that I was all set. Mom hugged me so tight while saying, "Momma loves you so much, and you can always come back home if you want." I cried a little when she said those words. I told her that I loved her too.

Immediately following her and I's interaction, there came a knock on the door. It was Daddy! My mother opened the door and asked him to come inside. She demanded that he take good care of me, and he promised he would. Daddy asked if I was ready to go, and I happily said yes. He proceeded to gather my belongings and placed them in the car as I said my final goodbyes. While pulling out of the driveway, my mother and siblings stood at the door, waving me off. I will never forget the look that my family had on that day. It was as if they would never see me again.

CHAPTER 13
Overjoyed

I t was just Daddy and me in the car headed to Toledo, Ohio. Before getting on the road, we made a few stops on the way to his side of the family's houses. Being around Daddy was such a high. He kept asking me what I wanted to eat, but I was full off of the excitement. I was ready to get out of Columbus as quickly as possible before my mom called and changed her mind. Daddy asked me to sit close to him while in the car, per usual. I slid over to the middle seat to be closer to him, and daddy put his arm around my shoulder as we drove. We sat smiling ear to ear while staring back at one another. Daddy asked if I could believe this was happening. I shook my head in amazement.

Toledo is about three hours from Columbus. After an hour on the road, we pulled over to rest and continued talking. I felt like a bird being released from the nest and learning how to fly. Daddy pulled me close and hugged me real tight while telling me he loved me. I smiled and hugged him back. Then, it happened. He began to kiss my forehead, then my nose, and finally my mouth. I pulled away from him a little, and he asked me if I was okay, and I said yes.

Daddy continued to tell me that it was a dream come true for him, and I felt the same way. He mentioned that his wives and other children were excited about my arrival as well. With tears in my eyes, with his tongue, Daddy started kissing me in the mouth again. I pulled back from him quickly. He expressed that he had been trying to control his emotions concerning me but had not been successful in doing so. I told him I'd help by continuing to pray a little harder for him, and he said thank you. Daddy started the car, and we got back on the highway headed to Toledo. On the rest of the ride, we sang a little, talked a lot, cried some, and laughed about how it came to be we were together.

It was terrific knowing Daddy had not abandoned me and knowing he had always wanted me to be in his life since birth. I continued thinking about appointments that required both my mother and father, but only my mother was there. People used to ask where my father was, and I would tell them I didn't know. I was thrilled to be living the dream which I never imagined would be a reality.

While driving, there was not one dull moment. I had so much fun looking at the beautiful trees, admiring the unique mosques we saw, and talking about everything we would do together as a family. Daddy told me I would have my own room, which was the most incredible news since sliced bread. I asked Daddy what kind of work he did, and he said, "A little bit of this and a little bit of that."

I asked, "What does that mean?"

Daddy looked at me and began to laugh, so I asked, "What's so funny?"

He shook his head and pinched my cheek. I was anxious to see what Toledo looked like as well as my new home. I looked forward to meeting my two little brothers and getting enrolled in school. It is unbelievable how one's life can change so fast.

As we drove, there were signs to tell us how close we were getting to Toledo, and at the same time, I was beginning to get a little hungry. So, we stopped at Cracker Barrel right outside of Toledo and grabbed a bite to eat. Daddy ordered for us both as I admired the different things that were in the restaurant. Back home, we didn't go out to eat much because of having such a large family and not a lot of money. However, I was already getting used to this new way of life and enjoyed all of the spoilings I received. As I finished my food, Daddy sat there on the other side of the table and just smiled at me with excitement in his eyes. He asked if I was ready to go, and as we headed out, he purchased some candy that he saw me admiring earlier.

Almost arriving in Toledo, I began to ask questions about the family's living arrangements in the home. Daddy informed me that he and his two wives slept in the same bedroom, and the children had their own rooms. He also let me know that he loved animals such as cats, dogs, fish, snakes, and lizards. I shrieked a little as he called the different animals because I was only used to a dog back home. Daddy thought that was funny and broke out into a loud giggle as if someone was tickling him. He told me not to worry because each animal had their perspective cages, which made me feel a little better. Finally, we got off at the Collingwood exit in Toledo, and I *really* became anxious to see my new home.

As we drove through downtown, it was tiny compared to downtown Columbus.

No one was even standing on the sidewalks, let alone driving through the little city. Ultimately, what the town looked like mattered none. All that mattered was me being with Daddy. The journey to arriving at Daddy's home was equal to Christmas morning, waiting to unwrap presents underneath the tree. We pulled up to this enormous house which ended up being my dad's aunt's home. Before opening my door, he informed me of some family that was there waiting to see me. When opening my door, he told me that a real gentleman should always open doors for ladies.

We entered the big doors of my aunt's home, and there were a handful of people standing around awaiting our arrival. If I'm honest, I felt like a celebrity that had just flown into town. Different ones began to introduce themselves and welcomed me to the family. As they told me their names, I knew that it would take a while before I could remember who was who. Everyone was stating how much I looked just like Daddy, even down to my bowed legs. As I looked into each one's face, I realized that we all looked alike, making me feel more of a part of the family.

The house was like a mansion, which had several rooms in it. There was also white carpet throughout the whole house with plastic on the furniture. The only time I'd seen something like that was on Big Valley or in magazines. So, seeing a mansion in person was mind-blowing.

Daddy was so proud to parade me around to his family and friends alike, and he would let them know right away that he was going to be very protective of me. More people arrived at the mansion with hugs and kisses, which became overwhelming, but I enjoyed every bit of it. I learned that the family had a home health care business where everyone held employment through my daddy's aunt. That was very impressive to me seeing a family business and seeing the benefits. It wasn't long before one of the family members asked me to sing. My daddy jumped on the piano; I cleared my throat and began to sing. After finishing, there were cheers, whistling, and clapping throughout the mansion. I thanked everyone for their kind words and immediately sat back down on the sofa. As the time grew later, it was finally time to leave the mansion and see my new home. Daddy and I said our goodbyes, and we returned to the car heading to my new address.

CHAPTER 14
My New Home

As we drove away from the big house and headed to Daddy's place I'd soon call home, I was excited, nervous, and scared at the same time. Living with my father was the first time I had ever been away from my mother and siblings. Fear tried to come over me, and I began to question if moving was the right thing. I think Daddy could tell what I felt because he grabbed me by the hand and asked me whether everything was okay, and I told him yes. Daddy began to encourage me that everything would be just fine. He continued saying it was meant for me to move in with him and my new family.

Before I knew it, the car slowed down, and we began to turn into a driveway. I asked if that was our house, and Daddy said it was. The house was a nice size, not quite as big as my aunt's house. As usual, Daddy got out of the car first and came around the other side to open the door for me. I began to take out my belongings, but Daddy told me that he would get them. As I headed toward the porch, two women waited at the door with two children. They all welcomed me to my new home with hugs and a smile. When I entered the living room, I was amazed to see a place that looked like a coordinated jungle. There were cages in corners, a cage on the television, under coffee tables, and last but not least, a small pond in the corner of the room. I sat down on the couch very slowly because about four cats were roaming around the house, which I was not used to seeing. Daddy began to laugh at my facial expressions because he said I had the strangest look on my face. There were baby snakes under the coffee table, lizards, a parrot in the corner, goldfish in the pond, and a ferret under another coffee table. I was a little shaken and wondered, Lord, what am I doing?

Daddy's first wife asked me if I was scared of animals, and I shook my head very hard and looked terrified. Everyone thought my actions were funny, and at the same time, the second wife reassured me that nothing was going to hurt me. My two little brothers were just adorable as they introduced themselves again. They were the age of six and seven years old. They were trying to carry my bags upstairs to my room but were unsuccessful. As I continued studying this new home, I noticed a massive piece of tree bark that sat on the coffee table. I asked Daddy what it was for, and he picked it up, turned it over, held it to his ear, and began to dial out. I had never seen a telephone like that ever before. The second wife said my father had created the whole living room and made the tree bark to fit the phone. Daddy told me that he was gifted, but he didn't tell me to what extreme.

Daddy and the second wife took me to my room as the first wife cooked dinner.

Of course, I was intrigued by how these two women functioned in the home and appeared very happy. Compared to the life I was accustomed to, this seemed very strange. As we went upstairs, the boys waited for me at the entrance of my room, excited for me to see it.

My eyes lit up when I walked into this beautiful room that had all wicker furniture in it. My bed was made so beautifully and was all mine. There were many perfumes on my dresser, and there were even clothes hanging in the closet for me. I could feel a huge smile coming across my face as I gazed at my little paradise of a room. Daddy was thrilled to see me so happy.

The second wife began to help me put up my belongings in the dresser and the closet. I saw so many clothes with price tags still on them, so I asked Daddy if they were mine, and he said yes, they were. How exciting it was to know they prepared for me to come and bought things they thought I would like. I sat on my bed, just swinging my legs and looking around to see if I was dreaming or not.

After a while, the second wife left Daddy and me in the room. He asked her to help with the preparation of dinner. As I held the teddy bear on my bed, Daddy closed the bedroom door and began to embrace me with tears in his eyes. I asked him what was the matter with him and he said that he was so happy I was there. I thanked him for wanting me to be in his life and for accepting me into his home. Before I could finish talking, Daddy began to kiss me and stuck his tongue in my mouth. I quickly pushed away, and again, he apologized and said that he just loved me so much that he could not help himself. I patted him on the back and told him that it was okay and not to cry about it. I took my shoes off and put them neatly in my closet. It was so lovely not to share, sleep with anyone, or do anybody's hair but my own.

It was time for dinner, so I went and washed my hands and headed downstairs.

Daddy pulled out my chair and sat me right beside him as both wives were bringing dinner to the table. The two boys took their place at the table, and once everyone was sitting down, Daddy began to say grace. As he prayed, he began to thank God for bringing his family together and blessing us to meet. When finishing, everyone began to pass the food around, and then we started to eat. The first wife asked me how the food was, and I told her that it was delicious. She began to smile and thank me.

The first wife was Caucasian and very pretty. The second wife was very sophisticated. As everyone was finishing up, I volunteered to do the dishes and the second wife said she would assist me. While cleaning the kitchen, I wondered what I was going to call the second wife. Daddy had already told me I could call the first wife Mom and the second wife by her first name. I wasn't comfortable with calling grownups by their first name, so it took a little time to say it. When we finished cleaning the kitchen, everyone went into the living room to watch television.

I moved a little slower into the living room, seeing that it was not my favorite place with all the wildlife staring at me. The boys lay on the floor, tapping on the cages while the cats ran around my feet. It was tough to concentrate on the television for fear that one of the baby snakes or lizards would get out. To make matters worse, Daddy opened up the lizard cage and took one out, set the lizard on his shoulder, and allowed the boys to pet the lizard. Immediately, I took off running, and everyone began to laugh at me as I strolled back to the room. Daddy assured me that he wouldn't let anything happen to me. I sat on the couch and watched as Daddy and the boys played with the lizards and the cats. Mom and the second wife continued giggling at my facial expressions as they sat on the sofa. My brothers were so cute, trying to get me to play with the cats. I finally gave in a little and petted the cats.

While settling in, trying to get used to my new home, my new family's climate felt strange but exciting. As the time grew later, I became tired, so I asked if I could take a bath and prepare for bed. Mom told me where the wash clothes and towels were then I went upstairs to run my bathwater. My brothers ran upstairs after me to show me their pajamas. As I entered the bathroom and closed the door, I began to get sad thinking about my family that I left back home. I was wondering what they were doing since I wasn't there anymore. A little tear began to fall as I stepped into the tub, but I quickly wiped my face and thought about all of the fun things that I would experience in my new home.

After getting dressed, I headed to my room, which I loved so much, and sat on the bed. The boys came and hugged me, said good night, and ran down the small hallway. I pulled back my cover and climbed into bed as Daddy knocked on my door and asked if he could come in. He sat on the side of the bed, held my hand, and asked me how I felt. I told him I felt good. Then, he kissed me on the cheek and tucked me into bed. Daddy said tomorrow we would work on getting enrolled in school. He kissed me again and closed the door behind him. I lay there in my new bed, looking up at the ceiling and saying my prayers at the same time. I began to thank God for my new family, for my family at home, and for blessing us to drive over the highway without any harm or danger.

Afterward, I turned over, lay there for about ten more minutes, and then I drifted off to sleep.

CHAPTER 15
My Life Changed

W hen morning came, the children's excitement woke me up as they prepared to go to school. I sat up in bed, and the boys greeted me with good morning hugs, and soon my daddy followed them. He asked me if I slept okay, and I told him that it was great as he gently kissed me on my forehead. Mom and the second wife said good morning and let me know breakfast was ready. I jumped out of bed, went to the bathroom, and went downstairs to eat breakfast. Daddy pulled out my chair at the table; I sat down and began to say grace over my food. Mom had fixed bacon, eggs, fried potatoes, toast, and jelly. I had never met a Caucasian lady who could cook as well as she did. Daddy was a big eater, and both women ensured he had plenty to eat and then some.

We discussed how good my bed was and went over things to be done that day.

Daddy mentioned he would take me shopping which I was very excited to hear. We were also going to enroll in school and pay a few bills. Once I finished breakfast, I went to take my shower and then got dressed for the day. The kids left for school. Mom went to work, and the other wife began to straighten up the house while Daddy and I prepared to leave.

Wife number two was a very sophisticated lady who would clean the house with high-heeled shoes and suitable clothing to match. I was used to seeing house clothes and shoes for those types of chores, but somehow, she managed very well. All house duties were complete, and it was now time to go.

It was a cold but beautiful day as I stared out of the window, looking at how small Toledo seemed compared to Columbus. I would be attending Libbey High School, which was near the house. The school was much larger than Linden McKinley. I was excited to start, but I needed my birth certificate, which was something that I didn't bring with me from Columbus. We planned to have my mother mail my important papers as soon as possible. From there, we did a little shopping and visited more relatives. As we drove around town, it was interesting to see how Daddy and the second wife interacted with each other. I was raised not to get into the grown folk's business. So, I was limited in things I wanted to ask concerning his relationships with the two women. My father's lifestyle was foreign to me, being raised around preachers all of my life. For the most part, I would pray for my daddy, realizing that we all have sinned and have come short of the glory of God.

Every ten minutes, Daddy would ask me if I was okay, and I would respond by saying yes. Seeing there were always multiple children back home, it felt strange to be the only child. However, I enjoyed being the center of attention. It seemed like the more attention that Daddy would give me, the second wife became more agitated. I began to focus on everything else as they continued their discussion and tried not to escalate during the conversation. After a while, Daddy asked if I was ready to eat lunch, so we stopped at a restaurant. It became clear Daddy's conversation with the second wife was a disagreement that showed no signs of being solved. However, Daddy tried hard to cover up the tension.

Once everyone finished lunch, we continued the rest of our day of running errands. It was almost time for the kids to come home from school, so we headed home to meet them. The boys were excited when they came home, and they had a lot to say, so I took the time to listen. It was time to complete our chores around the house by then, which wasn't much since we all began cleaning earlier in the day.

As the wives prepared for dinner, Daddy followed me to my room and began to inquire how I was settling into the home. I told him that I was adjusting quickly and couldn't wait to go to school. Daddy stared at me as I straightened up my room, so I asked him what he was thinking. He gave me a little grin but said nothing. As I returned downstairs, my step-mom asked me to assist her in setting the table and fixing my little brother's plate. The oldest brother didn't eat a lot, but the youngest enjoyed his food tremendously. The family sat down at the table, and each one talked about their day as we ate dinner.

My brothers talked about their day at school. They began to brag about all of the girlfriends they had accumulated throughout the day. Daddy would give my brothers advice on relationships (like they were old enough to understand). I found it very funny to listen to their excitement and plans for the next day when returning to school. As the evening grew late, my step-mom prepared for the following day by setting out the boys' clothes. Hearing the boys go on about their day at school made me more excited to start pending the paperwork from my mom.

I was the first to prepare for bed because I was a little tired. I said good night to everyone and then went to my room to straighten up some before bed. As I climbed into the bed, there was a knock at the door. It was Daddy, so I told him to come in. He said he came to say good night and make sure I was okay. I told him I was doing well and ready to sleep. So, Daddy kissed me on the forehead, but he had a strange look on his face. I asked him what was wrong, and he said that he had some things on his mind but not to worry.

I rolled over to sleep as Daddy turned off the light and left the room, closing the door behind him. It seemed like I had been sleeping for a few hours before a noise awakened me in my room. There was a night light in the corner. I went to look to see what was going on; I noticed that Daddy was lying on the floor beside my bed, sobbing. I asked him why he was crying and what he was doing on the floor. Daddy had been drinking a little because of the smell that filled my room when he began to talk. Daddy said he was feeling bad because of what he had been thinking about all day. I asked him what he was thinking. He responded by saying that all he could think about was having sex with me.

In amazement, I looked at him and questioned why he'd ever want to do that? He said that I looked older than I was, plus he wasn't around when I was growing up, so all he could see was a beautiful young lady before him, more than me being his daughter. Daddy said that he knew these thoughts were wrong, but he could not shake what he was feeling and thinking. I suggested he let me pray for him that those thoughts would disappear, and he agreed. After praying, he went back to his room, and I went back to sleep.

A few hours later, I woke up to Daddy laying in my bed and kissing me on my face. I asked him what he was doing, and he said he only wanted to make sure that I was safe. I thought, "Is this really happening?" as I turned over to face the window. I lay there holding my breath and hoping that he would get up, but Daddy didn't leave. I figured if I lay on my stomach, I would control the situation without him getting upset. But before I knew it, I felt his hands going underneath my gown and his pants coming down as he climbed on the back of me and began to move in a circular motion. I was scared, so I just lay there with my body very tense, squeezing my legs together and praying that he would stop.

As the morning continued, Daddy ended up penetrating me, to my surprise, and all that I could do was cry as I lay there in shock. Daddy tried comforting me as I buried my head in the pillow that I was clenching the whole time. He began to cry and apologize for what he had done. Daddy promised that he would never do it again as he sat up in the bed, pulling up his pants.

CHAPTER 16

Confused and Fearful

"He shall cover thee with his feathers, and under his wings shalt thou trust: his truth shall be thy shield and buckler. Thou shalt not be afraid for the terror by night; nor for the arrow that flieth by day; Nor for the pestilence that walketh in darkness; nor for the destruction that wasteth at noonday."

— PSALM 91:4-6

I could not go back to sleep after the events that morning. It took me a while to come out of my room for breakfast. My step-mom asked me when I was coming downstairs, and I told her that I would be down in a little while. In my mind, I wondered how I could face Daddy, my step-mom, and everyone else. I kept asking myself, "Why has this happened to me?" About five minutes later, Daddy knocked on the door and asked me if I was coming down. I told him that I was on my way. Still confused, I headed downstairs for breakfast with very few words to say. I ate my breakfast and returned to my room to get dressed for the day. My step-mom left for work, so Daddy, wife number two, and myself were still home. I could overhear Daddy and wife number two arguing about something. Considering what happened the night before, I didn't have the attention span to care. My grandfather's warning replayed in my head that day. I pondered on leaving, but I feared judgment if I returned.

The argument between them grew louder, and I could hear her ask him where he was most of the night. Daddy told her to shut up a few times, and when she didn't, suddenly I heard slapping and hitting with swearing and crying. I sat on my bed, grabbed the pillow, and began to pray while rocking back and forth. Soon, the noise faded away, and there was silence for a few hours. The next thing I heard was Daddy telling wife number two he would take her to Columbus to stay for good.

I hung out in my room until my brothers came home from school. They came in wanting to tell me everything that happened at school and how many girlfriends they had. I began to clean the kitchen because it was almost time for my step-mom to come home. Daddy came into the kitchen and asked me if I was okay. I shook my head yes without looking at him. So, he lifted my head and kissed me on the forehead. I continued to wash the dishes feeling very nervous on the inside. There was a lot of tension when my step-mom came home. She began to ask what was going on, but no one responded right away.

As I finished up the dishes, it was time to help prepare dinner for the evening. My step-mom was a terrific cook, and I loved to help her with the different meals she would prepare. The boys were crazy about their mom, and they would follow her around so that they could tell her about their day. My step-mom was a big cat lover, so it was challenging for me to help prepare meals with cats hanging out in the kitchen. Sometimes the cats would jump up on countertops, stoves, and tables where the food was. I would try to stop them as much as I could.

The family gathered in the living room to watch television, but I went to my room instead. I lay on my bed, still thinking about what had transpired last night through this morning. My brothers came upstairs to see what I was doing, then a few minutes after, Daddy came to ask me why I was in my room. I told him that I was tired and just wanted to be alone. By that time, my step-mom had called my name to help her with folding clothes. Step-mom asked how my day was. I responded by saying that it was fine. She just looked at me as if she did not believe me. I asked her if I could go and check to see if the mailman had come because I was waiting on the documents my mother was sending me for school.

I was so happy to see the mail with a Columbus address on it. I gave the rest of the mail to my step-mom and let Daddy know that my information had come for me to start school. Although I was feeling strange, I was excited about starting school. I went to my room and began to pick out what I would wear the following day.

As the time grew closer to evening, my mind couldn't help but wonder if there was going to be a repeat of the night before. I began to pray for God's protection and continued to prepare for my first day of school. High tension between wife number two and Daddy remained in the house. Step-mom was still asking what happened while she was at work. I could overhear them talking in their bedroom about Daddy taking wife number two back to Columbus to live. Wife number two was nice, but I could tell that she also had an issue with me. I couldn't help thinking she knew what had happened between myself and Daddy.

I just wanted to forget the incident and enroll in school the next day. I said good night to everyone and went to bed, eager for the morning to come. Seeing what happened the night before, it took a while before I finally dozed off to sleep. Morning came swift, and when the alarm went off, I jumped out of bed and headed to the shower. I was so excited that I didn't even want breakfast, but my step-mom suggested eating a little something. I ate a bowl of cereal after I had gotten dressed, then I waited for Daddy to get dressed to enroll me in school.

When we got into the car, Daddy asked me how I slept, and I told him that I slept well. He reached over and kissed me on the forehead. He told me that I looked pretty. I thanked him for the compliment as I slid closer to the door. Daddy then reached out his hand and put it on the back of the seat, but I kept staring out of the window. My school was within a ten-minute walking distance, but Daddy would not let me walk anywhere.

Here we were in front of Libbey High School, and it took everything in me not to skip into the building. Daddy stopped the car and opened the car door for me, and then we headed to the school's front door. It is always awkward when you start a new school because it seems like everyone is staring at you, trying to figure you out. I was already a shy person, and looking older than my age didn't help matters either. The process didn't take long because most of my scheduling had been completed before I came in. The counselor showed Daddy and me around the school, and afterward, I proceeded to go to my classes. Daddy kissed me on the cheek and told me to have a great day. He also gave me money for lunch.

As I went to each of my classes, the girls whispered, and the guys were whistling. Some students asked me if I was a new teacher. I responded by saying "no" with a bit of a giggle to follow. When going to school in Columbus, I only wore hand-me-downs. So, I felt pretty good as I strolled around in my new clothes and was not being teased. I enjoyed going to school, getting good grades, and helping the teachers by assisting in the cafeteria.

I was always on the honor roll every year. I enjoyed bringing home my certificates. At the end of the day, when it was time to go home, Daddy was waiting outside in front of the school to pick me up. I had met a few girls that day, and upon leaving, we discussed that we would sit by each other for lunch the next day.

I got into the car; Daddy and wife number two were in another heated discussion. Daddy paused to ask me how my day was, and I told him that it was fine. I couldn't wait to get home, seeing that things were getting worse between the two of them. Reluctantly, I spoke to wife number two, and she spoke back. She asked me if I enjoyed school, and I told her I did. My step-mom was at home cleaning, so when we arrived, I changed my clothes and began doing my chores. Wife number two hardly did a lot of cleaning up. She mostly stayed nicely dressed in heels and talked with my father most of the time with a drink in hand. As I assisted with dinner, Daddy watched me set the table, and he began to ask me what I did in school. I told him about each period, and he asked me if any guys had tried to hit on me. I told him they didn't.

CHAPTER 17
Losing Myself

*"Yea, though I **walk through the valley** of the shadow of death, I will fear no evil: for thou art with me; thy rod and thy staff **they** comfort me."*

— *PSALM* 23:4

I was excited to prepare for school the following day, so I took my shower early to go to bed on time. I picked out my clothes, said good night to everyone in the house, then went to bed. Libbey High School was the biggest school I had ever attended, and I was anxious to get into choir.

Sleep was good, then suddenly, I felt hands all over me again, so I slowly opened my eyes, and it was Daddy lying beside me. I wanted to scream and tell him to leave me alone, but I lay there cringing on the inside. Daddy began to move his lower body back and forth against my body, and I tried to move over, but he would pull me closer. He began to share that his sexual feelings were due to the shape of my body. He said he had been focusing on my shape since we met. As I continued to lay there, pulling the covers closer, Daddy climbed on top of me and began to kiss me on my face and neck. I asked him to please stop, but he continued to kiss me and feel all over my body. In minutes, Daddy had penetrated me despite my request. I lay there still, with tears in my eyes, and once he looked at me, Daddy began to beg for forgiveness. I looked at him, but I didn't respond right away. Daddy continued to cry and tell me how much he loved me and never hurt me.

It was time for me to get up and get ready for school, so I asked to be excused to go to the bathroom, and he allowed me to get up. As I ran to the bathroom to get into the shower, I cried silently as I began to wash. I took a shower longer than usual, just so no one would hear me crying as I pondered on what had happened. I felt like hiding under a rock because Daddy had told me that no one would know except me unless I told someone. As I dried off, I began to reassure myself that I'd be alright and not to worry because Daddy promised that it wouldn't happen again.

I got dressed, and Daddy was waiting on me so he could take me to school. It was a quiet ride to school on my end, but Daddy continued to ask me if I was okay and reminded me not to share what had been going on with anyone. I promised him that I would not as he held my hand while pulling up to the school. As I grabbed the car door, Daddy pulled me to him to kiss me on the cheek, and he told me to have a good day. I thanked him as I got out of the car heading into the building.

High school seemed to have had older-looking kids than middle school. At Libbey, there were a lot of Hispanics and Latinos as well as African-Americans and Caucasians. I was learning my way around the school fairly well while meeting more students along the way. Word got around the school fast that I could sing, so that would always be a topic of discussion. Most of the teachers were nice to me, although some students tried to discourage me from them.

My favorite subjects were music, art, writing, and reading. I hated math, social studies, and woodshop. As I went to each class and met other students, my thoughts remained scattered between learning and questioning what the night would bring when going to bed. I just wanted us to be a happy family and continue to grow together. Apart from me was thinking that maybe I *should* tell someone. Then another part of me feared judgment if I did tell. Most of all, I was afraid because I had never heard of or experienced anything like this before.

Some of the students would introduce themselves, and I would respond, but they could tell that I was distant even though I was friendly. As the end of the day grew closer, I began to get nervous but tried to reassure myself that I would be fine. The bell rang, and it was time to head to the lockers and exit the building. My father was waiting in the front and leaning against the car. As I approached, Daddy met me halfway and opened the door so that I could get into the car. He got into the car and leaned over to kiss me on the cheek. I was uneasy because we had not pulled away from the school yet. Daddy asked me how my day was, and I told him it was fine. He then asked if any boys were trying to flirt with me, and I said I didn't think so. I could tell that Daddy didn't like my answer because he began to laugh a little. Nothing else was said for the remainder of the ride, which was a little scary and unusual.

I jumped out of the car and went into the house to change my clothes and prepare to do chores. On the way upstairs, I spoke to my step-mom and asked how her day was going. She was playing with the cats on the living room floor. I changed my clothes, put my books on the bed, and came downstairs to clean the kitchen. It was my turn to fix dinner, so the food I was preparing was unthawed in the sink. Wife number two was sitting on the couch watching television with a drink in her hand. She wasn't thrilled, but she remained friendly. The following week, wife number two said her goodbyes and abruptly moved back to Columbus, Ohio.

CHAPTER 18
Brokenhearted

"The LORD is nigh unto them that are of a broken heart; and saveth such as be of a contrite spirit. Many are the afflictions of the righteous: but the LORD delivereth him out of them all."

— PSALM 34:18-19

As evening drew near, I began to prepare for school the following day before bed. My step-mom came into my room and asked me how things were going at school, and I told her school was going fine. She then asked if anything else was going on that I wanted to talk about, but I told her that nothing was going on. Inside, I was shaking, wondering if she had some idea about what Daddy had been doing.

My step-mom soon left the room so that I could prepare for bed. I climbed into bed, hoping that Daddy would pass my door and not come in. I heard Daddy and my stepmother arguing about something about an hour later. Next thing you know, I heard hitting and hollering. I crawled under the cover and began to rock myself to sleep. I would wake up periodically, and I could still hear arguing and fighting going on. I became terrified because the drinking and the fighting happened at least three times a week.

Around 4:00 a.m., Daddy came into the room and lay on my floor beside the bed, crying until I woke up. I asked him what was going on, and he responded saying he could not stop thinking about me and wanted to hold me in his arms. I sighed for a moment, then I asked him if he would try anything, and he promised that he wouldn't. So, I sat up, hugged Daddy, and patted him on the back. I tried to let go. But Daddy held on tight, sobbing, kissing my neck and cheek. Before I knew it, he had pulled me down off the bed to the floor and began to do what he said that he would not do. In my mind, I was fighting Daddy off of me, but in reality, I lay there wishing he would stop.

Once Daddy finished, it was almost time to get up, and there was no way I could go back to sleep. There I lay on my bed, in disbelief that my daddy continued to have sex with me against my will. Each time this invasion would happen, a piece of my heart would ache. More importantly, fragments of my innocence and childhood left my existence.

As I got ready to get in the shower, my mind couldn't help but wonder, "Why *me*?" I never thought in my wildest dreams that I would ever encounter this type of abuse. The strange thing about it all was that I still loved my father, but I didn't like what he was doing. Each time he would misuse me, I would become more fearful of him. When Daddy would become intoxicated, he would fight and bring up his horrifying past. He would always talk about being in the war. Daddy expressed that unfair people left him after all the love and care he'd continuously given. I would ask Daddy to pray concerning the problems that plagued him. Daddy would respond by saying he was unsure if God loved him or answered his prayers. Although it seemed strange, I would try to encourage him since he was a Bishop in his uncle's church.

Daddy was very knowledgeable concerning the Bible. He would love to get into debates about the word of God regularly. If anyone tried to use the Bible to condemn his choices, Daddy would tell them off quickly. Daddy's uncle, a Bishop, and other family members would sometimes address him about his ungodly lifestyle and even warn him of going to hell for his actions. However, fearing hell was the last thing on Daddy's list.

I was heartbroken at my father's lifestyle and actions toward me. When I first met him, I was proud that he was in church. But as time went on, I could tell Daddy was all about the title of a Bishop but had no interest in having a relationship with God.

Daddy loved being the "big man on campus" and loved to think of others as being jealous. He was proud that he had multiple women living under the same roof and took pride in being cared for by these women. Although our family church did not approve of his lifestyle, they still acknowledged him as a Bishop.

CHAPTER 19
The Shock

"Come unto me, all ye that labour and are heavy laden, and I will give you rest. Take my yoke upon you, and learn of me; for I am meek and lowly in heart: and ye shall find rest unto your souls. For my yoke is easy, and my burden is light."

— MATTHEW 11:28-30

I have always loved going to school and meeting new people since I was younger.

High school was exciting because you never knew what would happen from one day to another. Although I was quiet and stayed to myself, people would always want to be around me. It took me some time to get used to the kids doing grown-up things like smoking, drinking, and getting high while in school. So, when I would get home, I would discuss school and what was going on during the day.

Daddy would chuckle while I was explaining my day. He would frequently ask if anyone was trying to talk to me. I would respond by saying that guys would speak, but I wouldn't entertain the conversation.

Often when Daddy would pick me up from school, he would watch the guys and how they would react around me.

So, the following week, I was going to my classes as usual, and when I arrived at my third class, Daddy was sitting in the back of the classroom dressed up in a suit and tie. I almost passed out when I saw him because I knew his reason for being there. Not only did he stay for that period, but he would follow me around to all of my classes. He continued to do this at least three to four days a week. The teachers thought it was so lovely that my father was concerned about my education. The boys, however, hated it because Daddy would give them an evil eye while he was smiling at them. The girls would come up to me and ask me why my father was always at the school, and I would say he loved me, but inwardly I was cringing.

When I ran for homecoming queen, Daddy made all of my posters to advertise all over the school for people to vote for me, which was amazing to experience. I hardly ever missed school unless I was sick. I woke up cramping badly one day, but I assumed my cycle was coming on. But this cramping continued for almost two weeks, and no pain medicine would work. Little did I know that this would take a turn for the worst. When I got up for school the following day, I noticed I could hardly straighten upright and barely walk.

When my stepmother checked on me to see if I was getting ready for school, I told her about the pain I was experiencing. She then went and told Daddy. He knocked on my bedroom door and asked me what the matter was. I began to say to him that it was excruciating to straighten my body, and I began to cry.

The pain went on for a few days and grew worse by the minute. My step-mom suggested that I go to the emergency room to get checked out. Daddy did not want to take me, but I wasn't getting any better. I slowly got dressed, and we went to the hospital.

Once Daddy and I arrived, he went and got a wheelchair for me. We filled out all of the necessary paperwork and waited patiently to be seen by the doctor. As we waited, Daddy continued to ask me if I was acting sick to get out of school. I told him absolutely not.

Finally, they called my name, and we went back to the room. The nurse began to ask me a series of questions like when was my last menstrual, how many days did it last, had I had any injuries that might have caused my body not to straighten up, and I answered her to the best of my ability. She said that the doctor would be in to see me shortly. They began to run several tests that came back negative.

When the doctor returned to see me, he said that he didn't seem to know why my body was not straightening up. The doctor asked me if I had a boyfriend, and I quickly responded by saying, "No!" He said that the only test left to do was to take a pregnancy test. Inside I cringed, and Daddy looked terrified. Hesitantly, we agreed to have it done.

As we sat waiting for the test results to come in, my mind raced, and my heart was pounding as Daddy and I sat there in silence. The doctor slowly walked back into the room with the results. He let my father and I know that I was definitely pregnant. He explained the root of my pain was because the fetus was stuck in my tubes.

I was in complete shock so much until I became emotionally frozen. Daddy's face looked terrified. There was nothing that the doctor could do to help me straighten up, which made everything heard seem worse. Daddy asked if I could receive any medication to aid my pain. The doctor informed us that medicine would lessen my pain, but it would not assist me in better walking. So, they sent us home with a few pain meds and told me to set up an appointment with my doctor for further instructions.

As soon as we got into the car, I began to cry and panic out of control. Daddy tried to calm me down, but he was also a nervous wreck. I could not believe that I was pregnant by my own father. Based on how hard Daddy and I took the news, it would be even more challenging for us to explain it to my step-mom. Instead of going home, we went to the park to talk about the situation. While pulling out a bottle of gin, Daddy began to apologize for having sex with me. My initial response was to punch him in the face.

Instead, I just looked at him with a blank stare in my eyes. We both knew that once we told my step-mom, all hell would break loose.

CHAPTER 20
All Hell Breaks Loose

As we left the park in total silence, I was staring out of the window as my life was flashing before me. Daddy grabbed my hand and wept as we got closer to the house. The closer we got, I felt like my heart was going to explode from fear of what was to come.

Once we pulled into the driveway, it was already hard to walk, but my knees began to buckle due to my nervousness.

We got out of the car and went into the house, headed upstairs where my stepmom was, and I sat on the bed with shame and guilt.

My stepmom asked, "What did the doctor say?"

Daddy replied, "There is something we need to talk to you about."

So, she stopped doing what she was doing and sat on the bed next to me. I was shaking inside and began to sweat profusely. Daddy and I looked at each other and sighed at the same time. We must have been taking too long to speak because my stepmom frustratingly asked, "What is going on?!"

Daddy began by saying, "Don't get mad at what I am about to share with you." My stepmom replied with a few choice words while looking at Daddy and me.

Daddy began to tell her how the doctor said I was three weeks pregnant. My stepmom immediately looked at me and said, "Who have you been messing around with?" My mouth and tongue became numb, and all that I could do was look down at the floor.

Daddy interrupted, saying, "Hold on, there's more I need to say."

My stepmom responded by saying, "Okay, what?"

Daddy developed a slight smirk on his face. When this happened, it meant Daddy was getting upset. Nevertheless, he continued to say he had been sleeping with me. My stepmom jumped up off the bed and looked at both of us with rage, anger, and disappointment. She yelled, "Are you SERIOUS?!" Daddy told her to sit down and be quiet, but she refused and continued to say how upset she was. My stepmom asked me, "What would your family say and do if they found out about this?!" She then turned to Daddy and screamed, "If I had a daughter and you did this to her, I would kill you!"

By then, they were arguing and fighting as I sat there and cried. The arguing and fighting continued for about an hour as Daddy continued drinking. My two brothers began to cry and asked if their mom was okay, and Daddy told them to go back to their rooms and close the door. I wanted to run to my room and hide in the closet, but I knew better not to move, so I sat there and quietly prayed for them to stop fighting. Before it was over, my stepmom had bruises all over her, but she didn't seem to care.

Finally, Daddy excused me to go to my room, and I ran out of there as fast as I could, bent over and all. I felt so worthless, shameful, ugly, rejected by God, and sick simultaneously. I crawled up into a fetal position as the arguing and fighting continued, rocking myself back and forth, trying to process everything mentally. I didn't know what to do at fifteen years old. I wanted to call my mom, but I knew I couldn't tell her. Then the thought of suicide occurred, but I was scared that I would go to hell if I did. Not to mention this child inside of me: my emotions were all over the place, and no one was there to help me sort this out. I was too ashamed and guilty to pray because I felt like God would never forgive me for the mess I got myself into.

I lay there until I drifted off to sleep. Then Daddy came into the room and awakened me. By this time, he was sloppy drunk and continuously crying saying how sorry he was, and begged me not to leave him because he loved me. He said he would take care of everything if I trusted him and did what he told me. I let him know that I was scared of him and how he beat women. He continued begging me not to leave him, and Daddy told me that he would not do it again. I just stared at him, knowing in my heart that this behavior was not going to end anytime soon.

I asked if my stepmom was still mad at us, and he responded by saying that she would be fine. So, I asked him what we would do about the baby inside of me, and he asked me what I wanted to do. I told him that I wanted to keep the baby, and he frowned and said that would not be possible because the baby would look like a monster. Tears filled my eyes all over again because I knew that having an abortion was wrong in God's eyes too. Daddy said that I would have a hard time explaining to everyone how the baby got here and that he was trying to protect me from being mistreated.

So, the next few days, Daddy began to check into finding abortion clinics and gathering the money to pay for the procedure. There was a lot of tension, anger, and frustration in the house, and I did all I could not to cause any more problems for my stepmom. However, I knew that I couldn't avoid having a one-on-one conversation with her. I approached my stepmom when Daddy was not around and asked her if I could talk to her. She looked at me with a straight face, and I began to apologize for hurting her and told her it was not my plan to do this. She asked me how this happened, and I told her everything as I looked down at the floor. While explaining everything, I could see she became angry again, but I continued to speak. With tears in her eyes, she said, "I won't ever forgive you or your father for what has happened." I couldn't be upset about her response because I didn't forgive myself either. My stepmom continued to express her feelings, and I quietly listened because she had a right to feel how she felt.

Knowing my stepmom welcomed me into her home and resulted in such betrayal hurt me more than words could explain. I could see the hate and disgust in her eyes. I thought about returning home to Columbus, but I felt like I would shame my family. I decided to stay and try to make things right with my stepmom. I had made up in my mind that I would do anything that she told me to do from that day forward. I asked her if I could clean her house every day, but she didn't respond. So, I started looking for things to help her without communicating. I wasn't a good housekeeper, but I became better at it in time.

I hadn't been to school in a few weeks because I still couldn't walk. The next day, Daddy had set my appointment for the abortion, and I was scared and nervous. We arrived at the abortion clinic, and they took me to a room with a small table and a machine that looked like a vacuum cleaner beside it. The nurse told me to get undressed, put on a gown and get onto the table. After getting on the table, she told me to relax and breathe as they inserted the long tube into my private area. I began to cry and stare at the ceiling. I felt awful knowing what I was doing to my child. The nurse turned the machine on, and I felt pressure in my stomach. Within a few minutes, the procedure was complete. The nurse asked me to sit up and get dressed, then return to the waiting room where my father was.

After I got dressed, I noticed that I could stand upright again. As we got into the car, Daddy asked me if I was okay, and I told him that I didn't know how to feel. He reassured me that things would get better. Once we arrived back home, I spoke to my stepmom and went to bed because I was a bit crampy and mentally exhausted. I skipped dinner and prepared to go to school the next day. Daddy checked on me a few times and went back to his room, where I could still hear the two of them arguing. After getting my clothes out for school, I got back into bed, replaying the whole day over and over again. I was so amazed at how my body straightened back up. I called it my "Nebuchadnezzar experience."

CHAPTER 21
Trying to Drown Out the Pain

"There hath no temptation taken hold of you but such as is common to man. But God is faithful; He will not suffer you to be tempted beyond that which ye are able to bear, but with the temptation will also make a way to escape, that ye may be able to bear it."

— *1 CORINTHIANS 10:13*

As I returned to school, I had a few classmates ask why I had been absent and had to complete a lot of make-up work. I just told everyone that I was extremely ill but felt much better. While telling them, I felt highly broken on the inside. Although I looked like a regular teenager in school, I lived the life of what felt like a forty-year-old woman. Many of the kids were very open about their personal life and didn't seem to care what others thought about it. Some would come to school high or intoxicated from the night before, which became triggering for me, seeing that Daddy was always drunk.

My father would take me to the clubs with him and others once or twice a week, but I would have a pop or a wine cooler. School and my home life became more stressful by the day. I felt like I was losing myself more and more. I could not stop replaying the abortion that had taken place. The guilt and shame that consumed my mind became overwhelming.

Daddy was still coming to school to sit in class with me at least three times a week. His obsession became more intense by the day. His conversations of never hurting and sleeping with me had begun to fade away. Daddy continuously told me how much he loved me and never wanted to live without me. The relationship between me and my stepmom remained tough. I had no choice but to respect her feelings concerning me because Daddy changed his stance and made his intentions clear. He told my stepmom that he was in love with me, and our intimate relationship would not stop.

My father had a lot of alcohol and drugs in our home, and considering what I was going through, it didn't take long for me to start indulging in it all. Teachers and counselors loved me and often asked me if I was okay, and I would respond with a fake smile and let them know everything was fine. One of my coping skills was to sing or hum to myself. We are all musically inclined and gifted to play instruments on both sides of my family.

It was always first and foremost on my mind how to get my stepmom to at least like me, so I would go out of my way to try to do something that would make her happy. I thought my stepmom was so beautiful. So, I would compliment her on her clothes, hair, and make-up. A few times, Daddy would feel as if she was mistreating me and would say something or even hit my stepmom, which would scare me.

Throughout my time living with Daddy, he had never hit me. One day, he called my name, and I didn't respond quickly enough. When I finally came, he slapped me, grabbed me by the neck, and threw me against the wall until I saw stars. After Daddy saw that I was crying, he grabbed me and told me sorry. He explained he was under a lot of pressure and was afraid that I would leave him one day. Daddy asked if I would forgive him, and I said yes. He began to hug and kiss me.

I dreaded being with him, but I felt like I didn't have a choice but to let him do whatever he wanted. We frequently went to the clubs, motorcycle clubs, and blues shows. Sometimes, my stepmom and I would rotate, staying home taking care of the kids.

Whenever Daddy would go out, there were always at least three to four women with him at one time. He would buy Wild Irish Rose and weed before leaving the house.

This particular time when he asked if I wanted some, I told him yes. Well, I had never smoked anything before nor drank any strong drink. Although I was nervous about doing it, I proceeded to put the blunt to my lips and smoked it. I thought that my lungs were going to come up through my mouth and land on the floor! I guess I inhaled too long and almost passed out from the first hit. Daddy and my stepmom began to laugh like crazy as they told me to breathe. I couldn't believe that grass wrapped in what looked like toilet paper could carry such a "punch." When I tasted the red Wild Irish Rose, I felt a burning in my chest, and I thought God was punishing me instantly for all of the things I had done wrong. My stepmom laughed so hard at my reaction, and it made me laugh too because it was the first time in a while that she wasn't upset with me. Well, I was drunk and high by the time we reached the club. It also was my sixteenth birthday, so they ordered the biggest glass and filled it to the top. I had to be carried out of the club and thrown into the back seat that evening. I was so drunk; I believe I was talking to myself.

Even after all of the smoking and drinking, no matter how hard I tried to drown the memories and the pain of what I was living through, I could still feel it. It took me two days to sober up, considering that I had to spend the night in the bathroom after I got home. My stepmom checked on me, but she said I had turned into Chatty Cathy trying to cuss, which was hilarious, seeing that I didn't use cuss words. Daddy just chuckled and told me that I had finally become a grown-up. At that moment, I wished that I could go back to being the church girl that I once was. My grandfather's voice played in my head. I could hear him saying that I would go through hell if I moved in with my father. I just thought they didn't want me to leave Columbus, Ohio, because I was very much a part of the church, but I was beginning to see what my grandfather saw.

As the days continued, the stress of living grew more, and my desire to mask my pain grew larger. I started to smoke and drink regularly. Not only did we go to clubs, but we performed in them as well, so I would take the opportunity to indulge more as I performed on stage. We were known for singing the "Blues," which I got used to because it sounded like gospel music. In many of our shows, people would even request us to sing a few gospel songs, which we would do at the end of our set. Going from singing in a bar full of drunk people throughout the week to singing at church on Sunday mornings was a whole new world for me. We would also travel back and forth to Columbus, Ohio, to sing in clubs and churches. I walked in so much conviction and condemnation by living this way. I felt that I was too far gone to even pray for myself, which further persuaded me to indulge in drugs and alcohol to drown out what was drowning me.

CHAPTER 22

A Brush with Death

"Saying, Touch not mine anointed, and do my prophets no harm."

— *1 CHRONICLES 16:22*

Although I had just turned sixteen, I looked like I was twenty-one and felt like I was thirty-five, living a double life. Daddy continued attending my school at least two to three times a week to keep an eye on me. It was the last day of school for that year, and the regular schedule was that he would be parked in front of the school to take me home. Strangely, when I walked out of the school, I did not see the car. As I looked around for him, a guy ran up to me, wrapped his arms around my neck, and asked me if I wanted to go out with him. I immediately began to push him away, nervously looking around to see if Daddy saw what had happened. After the guy did this, I saw Daddy's car slowly pull out from a side street where he had never parked before. I immediately felt nauseous and weak in the knees discerning that he saw the guy with his arm around my neck.

I approached the car, trying to pull myself together as Daddy rolled down the window with this particular smirk on his face. I could tell that

I was in BIG trouble. I climbed into the car, said hello, and tried to tell him what had happened. He looked at me and said, "Okay." But somehow, I knew that this would not be the end of this conversation. Sweating profusely, I jumped out of the car and ran upstairs to my room when we arrived home. I spoke to my stepmom and the boys on the way, hoping no one would ask if anything was wrong.

As the evening progressed, my stepmom had somewhere to go, so Daddy let her drive the car, and she took the boys with her. He called me to come downstairs, and I found him sitting at the dining room table drinking Wild Irish Rose and making a sawed-off shotgun. I sat at the opposite side of the table, slowly asking him if he wanted something to eat. He declined by shaking his head. He told me to strip naked and sit back down. By then, my hands were clammy, and my stomach began to turn even more as I watched him polish this gun and place three bullets on the table. I sat and stared at him, trying not to breathe heavily for about fifteen minutes, and then he spoke and asked, "So you have been messing around on me, huh?"

I responded by saying, "No, Sir!" And he continued to drink his wine, polish the gun, and load the gun with one bullet.

Daddy kept this smirk on his face the whole hour and a half that we were sitting there and continued to talk about all of the women who had done him wrong no matter how good he had been to them. He would often cry while drinking and continued to say that he knew that I was planning to leave him for someone else. Seeing the terror in his eyes and hearing the anguish in his voice, I began to tell him that I wasn't planning anything of the sort, but he just continued to repeat himself. About thirty minutes later, Daddy stood up from the table, picked up the gun and his drink, and slowly approached me. My heart was pounding so loud that I could hardly breathe as I stood from my seat. Daddy sat down immediately in the chair that I was sitting in, and I instantly fell to my knees in horror about what was getting ready to happen next. He looked at me as I glared into his eyes of fury mixed with hate and love; I clenched my hands together and began to pray to God that he would not kill me. Daddy said, "Do not pray to God but pray to me because I am the one that is holding the gun." I began praying to him out loud as he spun the chamber. With the same smirk, Daddy said, "Let's play a game and see if the gun will go off or not." He pulled me closer to him between his legs, placed the gun to my forehead, took another drink, and pulled the trigger. I squeezed my eyes and hands together, crying, peeing myself.

The gun popped, but nothing happened, so he pulled the trigger twice more. However, the last time he pulled it, the bullet came out. It boomeranged off of my forehead and went into the couch in the back of me. Immediately, I fell to the ground in shock, and Daddy cussed and dropped the gun quickly. He then slapped me and told me to go upstairs and clean myself up. I slowly got up off the floor and ran up the stairs blindly as tears flooded my face. I was in amazement at how God had intervened between me and death that night. I could not believe what had just happened, looking into the mirror in the bathroom, expecting to see a mark or indent on my forehead. I turned on the shower, still bewildered. It felt like I was in the Twilight Zone.

After showering for what seemed to be twenty minutes, I went straight to my room and climbed under the covers, still fearful of what could happen throughout the rest of the night. I could hear some moving around from Daddy. Then I heard my stepmom pull up. By this time, Daddy was fully drunk and crying in their bedroom. My stepmom tried to have a conversation with him, but he did not have much to say to her or the boys.

Sometime throughout the night, Daddy came into my room, sat on the bed, stared at me, crying and telling me that he loved me. I looked at him slowly and said that I loved him too, hoping that nothing else would happen. He lay down beside me with his arm over my waist, and my insides began to shake. But he told me that he would not hurt me anymore and that he should never have put the gun to my head.

Daddy cried himself to sleep while I trembled under the cover. I eased my way out of the bed and hid in my closet for the rest of the night. I could not go to sleep at all. When closing my eyes, the only thing I saw was the gun going off on my head. As I sat on my shoes in the closet, I continuously contemplated going downstairs, getting a butcher knife, and stabbing him right in the heart. I heard so many voices in my head. Still, the one that stood out the most was God's voice telling me that "Vengeance is mine, and I will repay." So, I just sat there crying in silence for the remainder of the night until I heard him turning in the bed, and I went into the bathroom until I heard him go back into his room.

CHAPTER 23

The Proposal & Ceremony

"For let not that man think that he shall receive any thing of the Lord. A double minded man is unstable in all his ways."

— JAMES 1:7-8

L ife continued to get crazier as Daddy got more possessive concerning me, continually asking me if I was planning to leave him and buying me things to appease me. The nightmares about the shooting and the abortion persisted for a while with no signs of ceasing. I tried to hide my feelings as I attempted to exist in this game we call "life." I began to look to food as a comfort zone because my step-mom was an excellent cook, and being in the kitchen together was a way we bonded. I didn't have any friends that I could talk to. For this reason, a lot of my processing happened inwardly.

My step-mom would sometimes ask me how I felt about the relationship between my father and me. I would tell her how I never thought I would be in a situation like this. She also frequently asked how my mother and grandparents would feel if they knew. I would drop my head in shame when she asked. My step-mom loved my grandparents and respected them highly.

Daddy was a handyman and could fix almost anything in a house. His side of the family had rehabilitation homes that hired him to do maintenance on the properties around Toledo. Often, Daddy would have me accompany him to assist and mainly watch him work. He required that I wear a dress and heels so his work would be pleasurable. I was not allowed to wear undergarments to access whenever he desired easily. On several occasions, we would stop at various parks where I would have to model for him on park benches and tables with specific items like corncobs and baseball bats placed into my private parts as he sat in the car ejaculating himself. I was humiliated, embarrassed, and ashamed, but it was better to be obedient than suffer the consequences.

Many men would stop and gaze at me for hours at a time, shouting out sexual comments, whistling, and blowing their horns as they passed by. Daily, I was losing myself and my morals, feeling like I would never see the *"me"* I once was. As time went on, the perversion increased every week. We owned a dog, and Daddy trained the dog to be sexually attracted to me. He told me that he was obsessed with my body and desired me to have sex with the dog and a horse. Thank God the intercourse never happened with the animals, but the dog would repeatedly come near me and do humping gestures.

Daddy became more intense about making sure I would not leave him for someone else through the summer. So, one particular evening, he told me that he was planning a trip for us to go to Los Vegas for two weeks because he knew some people down there. It sounded like it would be fun, seeing that I had never been before. Going to Los Vegas would take three to four days to drive, so we began to prepare for the long trip ahead. Preparing for the trip allowed me to think about something else for a change.

The night before leaving Toledo, Daddy sat me down and told me that we would get married in Los Vegas at one of the chapels there. I asked him how this was possible, and he informed me there wouldn't be anyone taking blood tests. Daddy said he had an alias name that he went by, so no one would know we were related. I was speechless and didn't know what to say. However, I went along with it. After all, I felt trapped for life regardless.

It was very humid as we traveled those days. We stayed at hotels at night and continued to drive throughout the day until we reached our destination. It was something to see the sites as we traveled. The boys enjoyed it tremendously as they rode with the windows down, waiting in anticipation to arrive. We stopped to see the Grand Canyon, which was an incredible experience. While the drive was impressive, the thought of actually marrying my father stayed at the front of my mind. By this time, I was becoming numb to who I was and what I had become in the last few months. There were times when I wanted to kill myself, but I was too scared to carry out the task. I thought about running away, but Daddy told me if I ever left him, that he would find me and kill me. I truly desired to pray for myself, but I felt like I had gone too far for God to hear my prayers. I again decided to exist because I must have deserved what was to come.

It took us about three days to get to Vegas, and we were exhausted when arriving at the home we were staying. The humidity was high, and people were out everywhere. The neighborhood where we were was beautiful, with palm trees swaying in the slight wind that was blowing. The people we stayed with were very hospitable for our days. It was my first time being in what appeared to me as a mansion with so many different levels. I never dreamed I would be in Las Vegas, let alone stay in a mansion. We all did our share of unpacking the van and getting ourselves situated in the rooms we would sleep in. We had free reign in the home to eat whatever we wanted or walk through the house, but Daddy ensured that we did not overstep our welcome. We didn't go anywhere for two days due to the long drive there. We all slept in one great room, which was pretty cool, like a big slumber party.

Through the excitement of being in Vegas, I was nervous about marrying my father. We visited several casinos and drove down the streets day and night, looking at all of the lights and events taking place. There were slot machines in grocery stores and bathrooms. Daddy let us play the slot machines, and the rolling sounds were exhilarating. I never thought I would be so excited about seeing fruit lined up beside each other with lights flashing and coins falling out of the machines. This newfound activity was very addictive and expensive.

On that third day of being there was the day set for the marriage ceremony. I really cannot put into words how I felt that particular day. There were many small chapels everywhere to choose from. When arriving at one, they asked us for our IDs and birth certificates. Daddy and I filled out paperwork, and then they directed us to a sanctuary for the ceremony. The ceremony only took about five minutes, and it was over. I walked out of that chapel as my father's wife *and* daughter at the same time.

The reality of going through the marriage ceremony let me know I had lost my mind with no sign of getting it back. Immediately following, we went to a club to celebrate this momentous occasion with drinking and smoking. My happiness stood superficial while I was dying another death inside. I thought about what my mother would say and how God felt about the decision I had made. I felt like an undeserving scum of the earth. I tried to drink anything that would allow me to escape and suppress the pain of the life I had accepted.

CHAPTER 24
Seven Years Being Married

*"And the **peace** of God, which passeth all understanding, shall keep your hearts and minds through Christ Jesus."*

— PHILIPPIANS 4:7

Our vacation was over, and now it was time to take that long drive back to Ohio. Daddy, my stepmom, and I took turns driving for at least eight to nine hours at a time. We didn't stop at any hotels on the way back, but we stopped at rest stops for a while, then we got back on the road. It seemed like it took forever to get back home since the excitement had dwindled.

Once we arrived home, we unpacked and proceeded with life as usual. While Daddy was excited to call me his new wife to people who did not know I was his child, my stepmom had to adjust to this unique situation forced on her. I was going through the motions of not trying to lose the little bit of mind that I had left. Daddy had a motorcycle club. We also performed in nightclubs, motorcycle clubs, and churches in and out of town. We were well known for singing the blues, gospel music, dressing up, and riding motorcycles. Daddy also picked up three to four more wives throughout the years. People would marvel at how well we got along with each other in public, and Daddy loved the attention.

We hit the clubs at least six days a week, and we always went to church on Sundays no matter how late we stayed out the night before. There were times when a third wife was living in the same house with us, but the other wives would have their own homes. Those times were very intense for my stepmom because she never wanted to share her home, let alone her bed. When a third wife did stay in the house, it gave me a small break from being the wife. It allowed me to complete my daughter duties and be alone more. Those days would not last long because eventually, a fight or argument would break out, and the third woman would have to go back to her place.

Our drinking increased through the years, and our drug habit became financially straining. Domestic violence between Daddy and us became more frequent. Depending on Daddy's mood, some days would be okay, but others would be chaotic. A few of his wives were very assertive and weren't afraid to fight back. The fighting between Daddy and the other wives could last for hours at a time.

Everything about living with Daddy became extremely triggering. When living at home with my mom, I watched her go through domestic violence, but she never fought back. I reminded myself a lot like my mother because when Daddy would hit and choke me, I never fought back either. I would try to obey anything he would ask me to do and never talk back. I didn't receive as many beatdowns as the other wives did for these reasons.

The other wives could come and go as they please. Although they would get beat, he never chased them if they wanted to leave. He'd only find another wife to marry. I would internalize my pain by eating alone when it was my turn to babysit the kids throughout the week. Daddy was possessive over me and my body, so I would only eat small portions while he was around. The extreme sexual desires in Daddy grew tremendously throughout the years. I was so miserable that I tried to escape once by asking his aunt to help me leave, which was an awful idea that backfired terribly. She told Daddy what I was planning to do. After learning what I asked of his aunt, he beat me half of the night and told me he would kill me if I ever tried to leave him again.

I still attended school, but my grades slightly shifted from straight As to some Cs because of all the stress I experienced. I would find myself yearning to get to church and pray in hopes something miraculous would happen to Daddy, and he wouldn't desire me anymore. While at church one Sunday morning, the spirit of the Lord fell on me, and I danced. I had no idea the beat down that I would receive later that night. Daddy said I only shouted because I wanted men to look at my body. Needless to say, I never did that again. From that moment on, I never showed any emotion in church again.

Emotionally, I had hit an all-time low. I often told myself that I wasn't worth anything at all. Despite everything that was going on, my stepmom would talk to me, and we eventually became a support for each other. We enjoyed watching tv programs and sneaking food we wanted when Daddy would go out with the other wives and girlfriends. It was always my stepmom's desire to have a baby girl one day. She told Daddy that she was pregnant and ended up having a baby girl, and her child was so beautiful. She stole my heart, and I was so glad that I could be a big sister to her. The boys were also excited to have a baby sister in the house. She became my baby doll and my joy in a time I needed it the most. My baby sister drew my siblings and me closer than ever. When nothing else would make me smile, I could always count on them. In their eyes, I was somebody and highly valued. It was amazing how my baby sister could detect if I were unhappy. Once she could talk, she'd often kiss my face and hug me to comfort me. She'd always say things like, "You are not alone," and "We love you for who you are."

I graduated high school in 1985, which was an exciting day for me. Daddy rented a limousine for me to ride in the entire day while he had the motorcycle club to direct traffic. My mom and siblings came to Toledo and celebrated that day with me, which made it extra special. I tried to hide all of my pain so that my mother and siblings would not worry about me. I missed my mom and siblings so much. Daddy allowed me to send each of my siblings their own large box of toys for Christmas every year. It was a joy to do this as their big sister who lived out of town. After graduation, my first job was becoming a nurse's aide, where I took care of the elderly. It was hard work taking care of so many patients at one time. The pay was nice, but I did not get to keep any of the money that I made because everything went right to Daddy. I began working for Daddy's aunt, who had a business taking care of those who could not take care of themselves for a side job. That money went to Daddy as well. Daddy was still the maintenance guy for all of the properties, so he could show up at any given time to see what I was doing and make sure that I was not messing around on him behind his back. When I would go to work, I always thought about the day I would get away from my Daddy and this life that I was living. Although the thought terrified me, my mind would still imagine escaping and returning to Columbus, Ohio. I knew that I had to keep it to myself this time and continually regain Daddy's trust. So, I would constantly tell him that I would never leave him and that I was pleased to stay with him forever.

CHAPTER 25

The Great Master's Escape

"Confess your faults one to another, and pray one for another, that ye may be healed. The effectual fervent prayer of a righteous man availeth much."

— JAMES 5:16

My married life with Daddy continued to be an emotional ride as the years continued to come and go. Daddy's excessive drinking and his obsession with me continued to escalate daily. I never could be seen even looking at another male without being accused of trying to get with them. I had to appear emotionally detached from the world and could never talk to any man who ever talked to me.

While singing at clubs and events, many men would approach Daddy or me. They would ask Daddy if they could take me out on a date. He would respond by saying, "She's a grown woman. You are going to have to ask her." Daddy would be watching with a drink in his hand and a smirk on his face, giving me the "eye" that I better respond in the right way.

I contemplated suicide so many times. However, I knew that I would go to hell if I did. Plus, I was already living in a physical hell. Our lives were very repetitive week by week with nothing new, making life even worse. We'd go to work in the daytime, go clubbing in the evenings or riding motorcycles, get drunk and high, then go to church on Sundays only to get out of service and return to the clubs afterward. While working, I could meditate on what I wanted my life to become despite my present reality. There was a constant state of chaos at home, making it impossible to obtain any peace. More and more, I began to miss my mother and family. I could literally feel my mother and grandmother's prayers concerning me. I would find myself subconsciously praying, asking God to please deliver me and not let me live the rest of my life in this misery I chose for myself.

In 2000, Daddy found another girlfriend to be a potential wife. Out of all the others, she and I seemed to have had a special bond. She was like an older sister that I never had. Although I had never shared anything with her, it was as though she could see straight through me. She had her own place but would come over at least three or four times a week. She and my stepmom didn't get along too well, but they were cordial while being around each other. She wasn't afraid to vocalize her opinions and views, which would get her into a lot of trouble with Daddy.

One day, she had a drink in her hand, and she began to ask Daddy why I did not have a boyfriend and why he did not let me go out with friends. Her tone while asking these questions was very rhetorical and sarcastic, which got her cussed out and beaten. I could not believe she stood up to Daddy concerning me and was not afraid to fight back. I had never seen a woman fight a man as she did. Several times, this would occur between the two of them over her strong comments. I admired her strength and ability to stand firm on what she believed. She'd often slide me a little bit of money, and I would hide it to buy something later. She would also whisper in my ear when Daddy wasn't looking that she would be willing to listen if I ever wanted to talk. I kept that message hidden in my heart.

After a while, when I'd go to work, I started calling my mom back home.

Although I'd try to appear calm and put together, she'd say, "I know you are unhappy, but I have been praying that God will bring you back home." Fear arrested the words I desired to say to her, and all I could do was cry. She'd also say, "I know you cannot share with me what is going on, but Jesus, the Master, knows everything." I would thank her for praying for me and reassure her that I'd call again. Mom brought so much peace and joy to me, giving me a little more strength to carry on.

As I would call her weekly while at work, I began to share that I was ready to come back home. My mom suggested that I hop on a bus, but I told her that I had no money. Slowly, she began to send me little gifts in the mail that had money hidden in them. It still wasn't enough for me to purchase a ticket, and honestly, I was scared to try to get one without Daddy finding out about it. I knew I had to obtain more funds to start my escape plan. So, I took advantage of Daddy's state of being excessively intoxicated. Once I knew he was drunk, I would sneak in his pockets after falling asleep and take two to three dollars. My mom began to tell me to start paying tithes on whatever funds I got my hands on.

While at work, I mailed the money for my tithes back to Columbus, Ohio. Mom said that by doing this, Jesus, The Master, would give us a plan and strategy to help me escape. When calling my mother the following week, she told me that she had spoken with one of my aunts. My aunt told my mother that her husband was willing to come to Toledo and get me. As exciting as it was to hear, I told her it would be too dangerous for him to come because Daddy would have tried to harm him. Mom understood and said, "We will keep praying until The Master gives us the answer," and got off of the phone.

I spent the next few days replaying the conversation my mother and I held. I also kept thinking about how Daddy's new girlfriend told me I could talk to her about anything, anytime. I felt ready to take her up on that offer. I could not wait to get back to work to sneak and call her. As soon as Daddy dropped me off, I ran to work, completed my tasks for the day, and immediately jumped on the phone to call Daddy's girlfriend.

She answered on the first ring, and my heart skipped a beat with excitement and fear all at once. I began to share what had been going on for years, and she began to sob. She told me to tell her exactly what she needed to do to help me get out. I told her what my mother and I had discussed concerning my aunt's husband. She said she would be willing to pick me up and take me halfway to Columbus, Ohio, if my aunt and uncle met us in Upper Sandusky.

I could not believe what I was hearing, but she assured me that she would not tell my father and we could do it on a day when it was my turn to babysit and Daddy and stepmom were gone. Daddy and my stepmom had a set evening to go on a weekly date. As nervous as I was, I called my mother and told her the plan. Mom called me right back and told me everything was ready to go.

I was happy and sad at the same time. Leaving while babysitting would be the second time I felt I had abandoned a set of siblings, and they were too young to be left alone. I began to question Jesus, the Master, if this was his plan of escape for me, and The Lord assured me that He would protect the children and no harm would come to them while they were left alone. Hearing Jesus say this to me brought me great peace in a time of major affliction.

It was time for me to become strategic in every move I made going forward.

Every step taken had to be aimed toward a clean escape. It was routine on Saturdays that we would go to the laundry mat. We would always use trash bags to put our clean laundry in. Once returning home from the laundry mat, this time, I added the other clothes I would take with me and put them in the closet instead of taking my laundry out of the bag.

The closer it got to my escape, the more fear took over. I started second-guessing every decision in fear of getting caught and not being able to leave Daddy. However, the Master reassured me to trust Him. Every Tuesday was the day Daddy and my stepmom went for their dates. That Tuesday evening came, and Daddy and stepmom went out like clockwork. As soon as they left the driveway, I called Daddy's girlfriend, and it took her ten minutes to get there. I told my siblings that I was going to take the trash out. In reality, the "trash" was all of my clothes and belongings.

I turned their favorite video on and told them that I would be right back, knowing I would not. How my heart loved my siblings and ached at me having to leave them, but it was time for me to reclaim my life. I proceeded to take out the four big trash bags and went out to put them in Daddy's girlfriend's car. As I looked back at the house, my siblings were standing in the window watching us. The look on their faces was as though they knew that was goodbye. We immediately pulled off and hit the highway. I spent the whole ride looking behind us, hoping that Daddy would not somehow find and follow us.

It took about an hour and a half before we got to Upper Sandusky. When arriving, my aunt and her husband were there waiting on me.

Seven years, I had been in hell for seven years. If you had told me a small conversation with Cassandra about finding my father led me to *this?* Oh, the things I would have done differently. However, *saying,* "I would have done things differently," I was warned several times. And yet, I ignored every warning out of greed for my own will. At twelve years old, I had made up in my mind that *I* knew what was best for me. Boy! Was I wrong?! Through the seven years, my mind had gone to a hollow place. I signed up for being raped to beaten, experiencing a brush with death, addicted to drugs and alcohol. What a lesson life has taught me. Healing has been a journey of trial and error. And no, I didn't know the full magnitude of what I got myself into. However, I only knew one person who could get me out, the Master.

After arriving in Sandusky, I hugged Daddy's girlfriend real tight and thanked her for everything she had done for me. My auntie and uncle thanked her for bringing me, and then we pulled off and headed home, my *real* home. I was thrilled, nervous, and at peace simultaneously. For the most part, I was quiet during the drive home, but my aunt was ecstatic. My uncle remained calm and collected while driving me to my grandmother's house, where my mother and siblings were waiting on me. When walking into my grandmother's home, the first person I saw was Mom. I ran to her in tears. She embraced me and said, "Jesus, The Master has brought you back in one piece."

About the Author

Sylvia Benson is...

instagram.com/ladysyl2u

www.ingramcontent.com/pod-product-compliance
Lightning Source LLC
Chambersburg PA
CBHW071016120626
46546CB00003B/1105